The Woodcuts of Harlan Hubbard

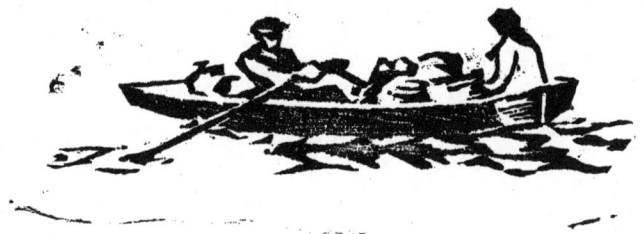

THE WOODCUTS OF HARLAN HUBBARD

From the Collection of Bill Caddell

With a Foreword by
Wendell Berry

THE UNIVERSITY PRESS OF KENTUCKY

Publication of this work was made possible by a grant
from the Mary and Barry Bingham, Sr. Fund.

Published by The University Press of Kentucky

Scholarly publisher for the Commonwealth,
serving Bellarmine College, Berea College, Centre
College of Kentucky, Eastern Kentucky University,
The Filson Club, Georgetown College, Kentucky
Historical Society, Kentucky State University,
Morehead State University, Murray State University,
Northern Kentucky University, Transylvania University,
University of Kentucky, University of Louisville,
and Western Kentucky University.

Editorial and Sales Offices: Lexington, Kentucky 40508-4008

Library of Congress Cataloging-in-Publication Data

Hubbard, Harlan.
    The woodcuts of Harlan Hubbard : from the collection of Bill
Caddell / with a foreword by Wendell Berry.
        p.   cm.
    ISBN 0-8131-1879-4
    1. Hubbard, Harlan—Catalogs.   2. Caddell, Bill—Art collections—
Catalogs.   3. Wood-engraving—Private collections—Indiana—Catalogs.   I. Title.
NE1112.H79A4   1994
769.92—dc20   94-13331

Contents

Publisher's Note

The 83 woodcuts included in this volume constitute nearly half of the prints Harlan Hubbard is known to have created in the course of his life. They were chosen not only for their esthetic appeal but also for the light they shed on the work of this important artist and writer. Works from Hubbard's earliest years as a printmaker are here, most never before published. Many of the prints from the shantyboat years (1944-51) and some from the Payne Hollow years (1952 on) have appeared in Hubbard's published books and other works, but often in reduced size. Most of his color prints are published here for the first time, all for the first time in color.

In 1987, Harlan Hubbard compiled a list of prints for a possible exhibit (shown in the footnotes to the prints as HH list). On it he indicated with one or two stars those he considered his better and best prints. The footnotes indicate which prints were on the list and which received stars, along with other comments by Hubbard on particular prints. (It should be noted that seventy or more prints had not at that time been collected and were thus not among those Hubbard considered.)

Also indicated in the footnotes are instances in which prints were produced from Hubbard's blocks by someone other than Hubbard; dimensions for prints reproduced here at a smaller size than the original; notes on the color(s) if reproduced here differently from the original (see Robert Browning Reed's essay below for discussion of the production of gray tones); additional notes on the dating; and notations of handwriting (presumably by Harlan Hubbard) on the print.

The chronological order of the prints cannot be determined. Hubbard rarely indicated a date on a print, with the exception of a few of the Christmas cards. (Some of the cards he hand dated at a later time.) Some prints can be dated approximately by the subject or place, especially those relating to the shantyboat years, but even this dating is uncertain, since he may have made the actual prints at a later time. Readers of *Payne Hollow*, for example, will notice that several woodcuts included here depict the same scenes as drawings included in that book. Which came first cannot be known, though it seems likely that the drawings were made quickly on the spot, the woodcuts, more laborious to produce, at a later date. Other clues to the dating might be found by a knowledgeable art historian in considerations of style and paper type, but again, these are uncertain evidence. Except for the few known to be very early, the arrangement of the prints here is largely arbitrary.

All works are reproduced at their original dimensions except for a few that could not be accommodated in a book of this size, and all but a handful are photographed from Hubbard's own prints. Exceptions are indicated in the footnotes.

With rare exceptions, Hubbard provided no titles for his woodcuts. The titles given here are merely indications of subject matter. The quotations accompanying the prints are from Hubbard's writings, but in only a few instances do they represent Hubbard's own statement about the particular print. They have been chosen to provide a link between Hubbard's writings and these visual representations of his long and thoughtful life.

Several people deserve thanks for making this book possible. Bill Caddell, Hubbard's artistic executor, proposed its publication and made available the prints from his extensive collection. Harriet Fowler, director of the University of Kentucky Art Museum, and artist Konrad Juestel of Valparaiso, Indiana, assisted with selection. Wendell Berry, in his Foreword, and Robert Browning Reed, in his examination of Hubbard's technique as a printmaker, help to place his work in the context of his life, his philosophy, and his stature as an artist. Florence Fowler Burdine selected the quotations from Hubbard's voluminous writings, both published and unpublished. A generous grant from the Mary and Barry Bingham, Sr. Fund made possible the inclusion of the color plates.

Foreword

During his working life as an artist, Harlan Hubbard's ruling passion—his obsession, one might almost say—was painting. That the world is colorful is the loveliest result of its illumination, and Harlan thought the light a daily blessing. He took great joy in the lights, forms, and colors of the world; in his art he meant to express his joy in these things and his thankfulness for his joy.

Harlan's was a life lived as much as possible outdoors, doing for himself the fundamental work of human life in this world: building shelter, growing or gathering food, cutting firewood. His early years were spent roaming the countryside of northern Kentucky and canoeing the Ohio River and its tributaries. In 1944, the year after his marriage to Anna Eikenhout, he built a shantyboat at Brent, Kentucky, near Fort Thomas, and he and Anna made an unhurried voyage that, beginning in Brent, ended in the bayous west of New Orleans in 1951. From 1952 until Anna's death in 1986 and Harlan's in 1988, they lived at Payne Hollow, on the river and well away from the road, in Trimble County, Kentucky. Throughout all these years and adventures, Harlan painted and made prints. In his journal he recorded his struggle: his elation, frustration, bewilderment, insight, success, failure, sometimes his despair, and his inevitably returning hope and curiosity and enthusiasm.

The journal, which says much about painting, says almost nothing about the making of woodblock prints.

Harlan seems, nevertheless, to have printed from woodblocks, off and on, throughout his life; he had made about 180 of them by the time of his death. Because he said so little about printmaking, his interest in this medium cannot be so clear to us as his interest in painting. Still, it is possible to make a few suppositions that are not entirely guesswork.

In addition to all else that he was, Harlan was a scavenger. He delighted in finding useful things in drift piles, in junk piles, or floating in the river. And he delighted in finding uses for the things he found. It is easy to imagine his pleasure in carving a design into a block of wood that someone else had thought worthless and thrown away. The scavenger thus became a salvager, a redeemer of sorts. And this, in miniature, is the story of Harlan's life, which was a saving and putting to use of what nobody else wanted.

Because he lived outside the "art world" and was mostly unknown as an artist, printmaking was the only means he had of reproducing and disseminating his work. For years his and Anna's Christmas card would be a small woodblock print, showing something of their life in something of Harlan's work.

But printmaking must also have been useful to his painting. For the most part it set him free of color, and so it may have permitted him to encounter more directly the issues of form. The enforced austerity of carved rather than drawn or painted shapes may have worked to the same end. At any rate, Harlan's prints give us a more spare and strictly formal version of his world than we find in the paintings, and from the prints we learn much of value about both the artist and his work.

His world, as the prints represent it, almost characteristically begins at the surface of a river, most often the Ohio. The river gives to vision a sort of absolute floor, which is yet fluid and transient, which is reflective and yet is a breaker and distorter of reflections.

And the sky gives to vision an absolute ceiling, formless in itself, and yet essential to the formality of the world. It is insubstantial, unsolid, and yet is ever-present, more lasting than any of the forms it contains: cloud or plume of smoke, hill or house or tree.

Between the river and the sky the shapes of earth and human work rise up and cast their shadows and reflections.

Of this world, Harlan in his art asked a few simple, endlessly fascinating, never definitively answerable questions.

What is the influence of the broad, moving plane of the river's surface upon the surrounding landscape? Upon boats moving over it? Upon the people in the boats?

How do the earth and its various creatures lift their forms up against the sky? How do these forms influence one another? How do light and substance make form?

How do houses and the other buildings of farmstead and village settle themselves into the landscape, among hills and trees?

How do tree branches hold light? How do they hold snow?

In the prints, as rarely in the paintings, he asked also, How is the human body shaped by effort? How is it shaped by rest? Some of these human images—of a man rowing a boat, or a man hammering, or a man sawing a log—appear to be self-portraits done, not from a mirror-image, but from his interior knowledge of his body.

And nowhere so much as in the prints does Harlan register the charm of boats: their shapes dictated by fluidity, motion, necessity, use; their pleasantness as idea and possibility; their floatability. One feels how much he loved to execute the line along the water's surface that defined their buoyancy. They are buildings, dwellings, suspended on water, and thus they become the key to a sort of metaphorical system in Harlan's work, in which all shapes—of water, earth, sky, and light—are analogues of one another, all fluid, all in motion.

Harlan's profoundest calling was to see in these transient shapes some enduring clarity of form and relationship, to trace out the lineaments of a timelessness in time and of the heavenly here on earth.

WENDELL BERRY

Harlan Hubbard as Printmaker

Throughout his life, although he painted in oil, acrylic, and watercolor, Harlan Hubbard also made many woodcuts, about 180 known examples. In his journals he frequently refers to his painting—his difficulties in achieving the results he desires and his distress at the recognition that eludes him in his chosen course. But only rarely does he speak of his prints, aside from occasional remarks such as "made two small oils, several watercolors and designed and carved a woodblock" (Journal, December 8, 1934).

Hubbard's prints display the same interests as much of his writing—the world of the river and its boats, the sky, trees, and hills. Although human habitations and figures appear in some of his prints, he rarely does a portrait, and still lifes are even rarer. Landscapes, riverscapes, and boats are his major subjects.

Woodcut is a form of relief printmaking in which the artist first draws his design on the wooden plank or transfers his drawing from paper, then cuts away the surface areas intended to remain ink-free, leaving in relief those areas intended to receive ink. The block is then inked, paper is laid on the block, and pressure is applied, using anything from a spoon, manipulated by handrubbing on the back of the paper, to a printing press.

Hubbard's woodcuts range in size from very small (about 1 ¼" square) to fairly large (10" x 13"). Sometimes he used one block of wood for several cuts, dividing the surface of the plank into sections. Occasionally he used both sides. His wood was obviously sal-vaged from flotsam and discards. I have examined a block cut from cedar siding, a soft wood that yields a fairly rough impression, and others made from hard woods such as birch. One block is a section of tree trunk, half round, with bark still attached on the back. Finer detail can be obtained from hard woods, which do not chip or splinter as easily as softer woods and which permit cutting in any direction with the V-shaped, or parting, tool. Hubbard obviously used the woodcut knife for much of his carving, though some of his blocks show evidence of gouge and chisel work. On rare occasions he exploits the texture of the wood to provide an interesting background, as in Prints 10 and 27.

Among Hubbard's papers and effects is a pamphlet on Japanese printmaking methods that may have had some influence on his way of working. Although he rarely exhibited other artists' work at Payne Hollow, he did have reproductions of Ukiyo-e by Hiroshige and other Japanese printmakers pinned up in his studio, along with an old Japanese watercolor scroll. Japanese printmakers have traditionally used a brush to apply ink, in contrast to Western printmakers, who usually ink with a small roller, or brayer. Hubbard may sometimes have inked his blocks with a brush—not surprising in one with his convictions about the use of materials and processes. The residues on the specimens I have seen appear not to have been caused by a brayer.

I am unable to determine what kind of ink

Hubbard used. Available inks are either oil- or water-based. Many of his papers appear to be Japanese, though I cannot tell which varieties. Bill Cadell tells me he brought Hubbard Hosho and Mitsumato papers (made from mulberry bark) from Japan. The slight bleeding that occurs with such a soft paper as Hosho, possibly used for Prints 55 and 60, may have appealed to Hubbard. Some of the harder papers he used may be American cover stock.

One of the problems for the woodcut artist is how to show gray areas. The cut block is usually printed with dark ink against a light background. To achieve gray tones from a single impression, the artist ordinarily uses a pattern of closely spaced parallel lines or occasionally dots or gouges, as Hubbard does in Prints 17, 50, and 69, or cuts with a V-shaped tool, as in Prints 2 and 46. Sometimes Hubbard creates an extremely delicate gray, possibly by use of very light pressure on the back of the paper, as in Prints 9 and 13. On other occasions he creates gray areas by use of gray ink on a separate block, as with Print 45. Generally we see a balance—white areas containing black line and black areas containing white line, as in Prints 48 and 65. Overall he shows great sensitivity to light and dark values, repeatedly playing black line against gray areas to create mood and to indicate season or time of day.

Hubbard printed most of his woodcuts in one color, usually black, but occasionally he ventured into color printing. His color prints exhibit a fairly narrow range of colors but achieve sometimes striking images, as in Plate IV, or very delicate ones, as in Plate III. To create a print of two or more colors, the artist cuts a key block. Prints from this block are offset on other blocks and all non-printing areas are cut away, leaving only the areas to be printed in the other colors. Each color is then successively printed on the paper, with the key block printed last, in black, to tie together the design.

A few Hubbard prints employ white ink. In Print 73, for example, the goats in the foreground are printed in white against dark green paper, while through the small window we see the reverse, dark against white. Others, such as Plates I and V and Print 36, use white ink against a light background for an extremely delicate effect—snow in two cases, smoke in one—an effect impossible to duplicate in standard four-color printing, as is used here.

Harlan Hubbard's woodcuts show considerable skill in use of the medium, an understanding and attention to composition, a desire for simplicity and direct expression free of petty detail, and a perception of abstract form. Studying them may help the reader to an appreciation of the work of this unique and valuable artist.

ROBERT BROWNING REED

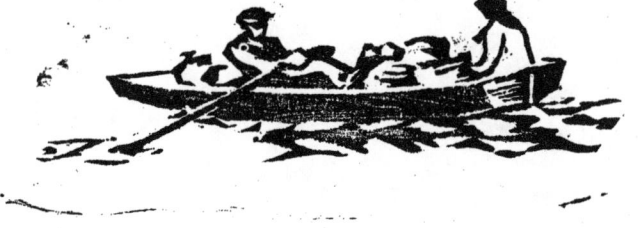

1 East River, 1925

In 1915, after I had been through one year of high school in Bellevue, my mother acceded to the wishes of her two older sons and moved to New York City. . . . During the months when I attended the National Academy of Design, my pedestrian excursions were in Manhattan, where I ranged the waterfront and the colorful streets of the East Side.

Journals, 1929-1944, pages 4, 7

Two stars on HH list. A note found with Hubbard's print says this was his first print; see also Plate I.

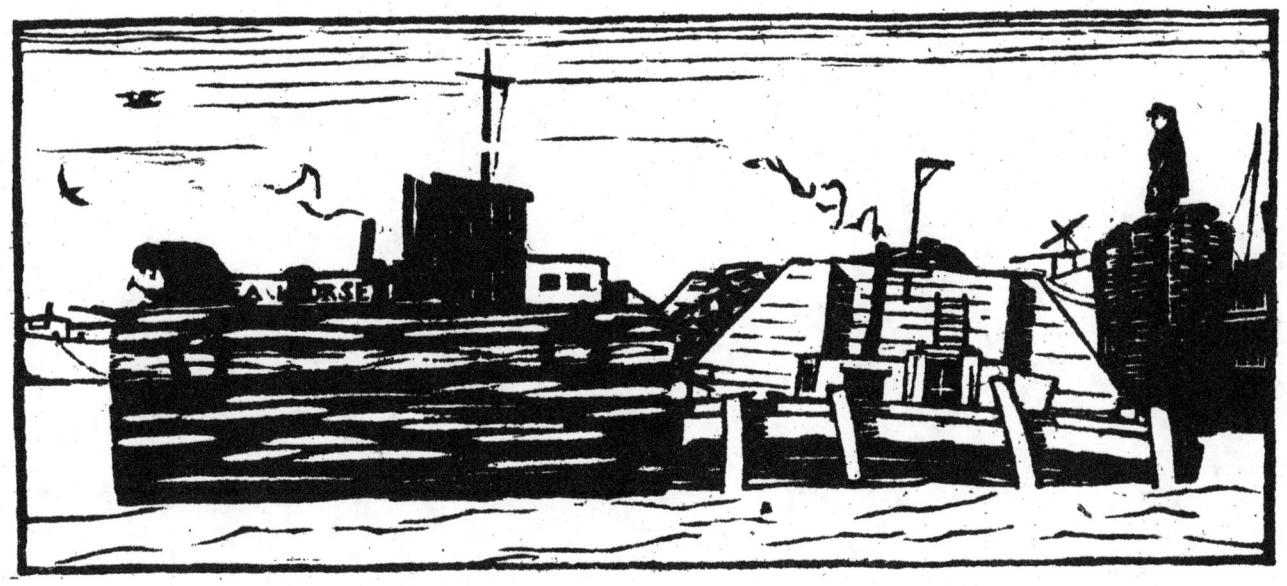

2 New York street scene

On HH list. One of Hubbard's earliest prints.
"NY" handwritten in pencil.

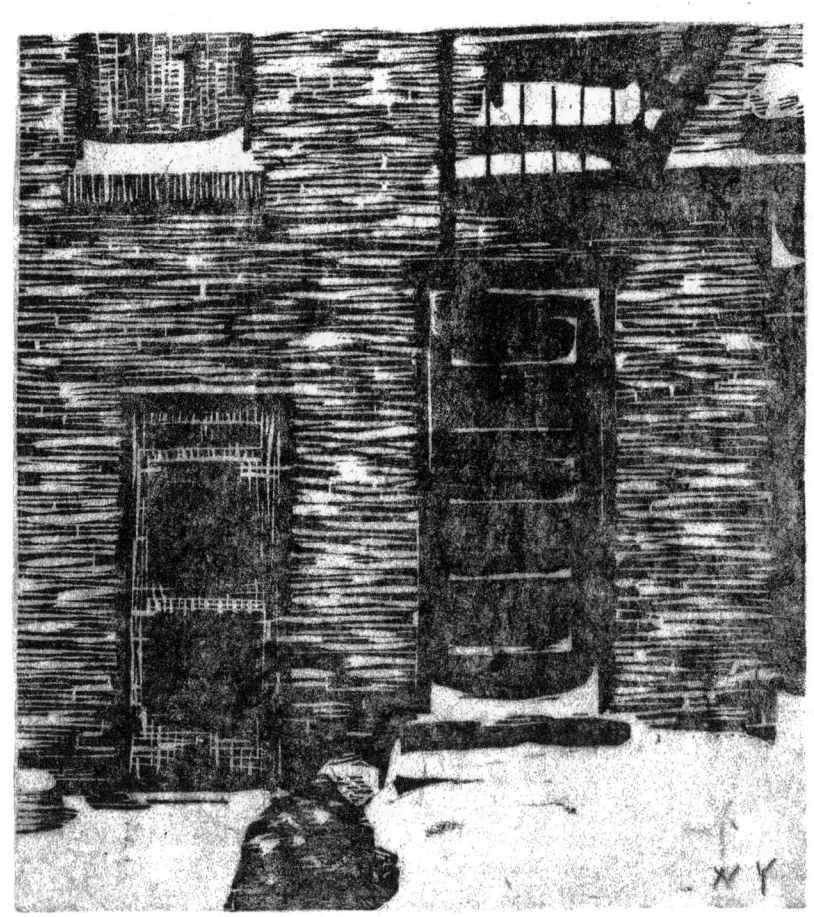

3   Skyline with houses

One of Hubbard's earliest prints.

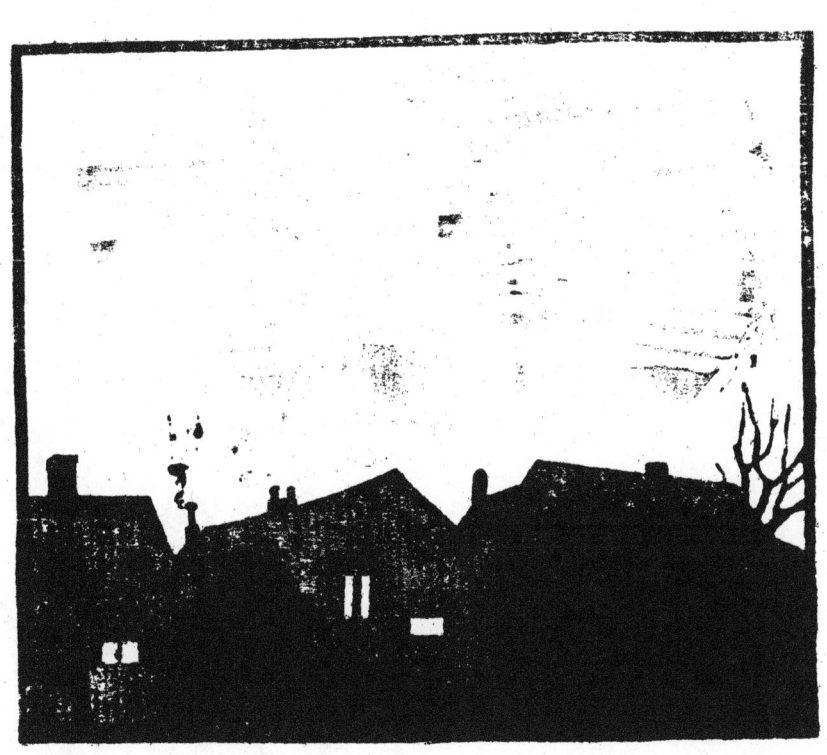

4   Catskill Mountains

One star on HH list.

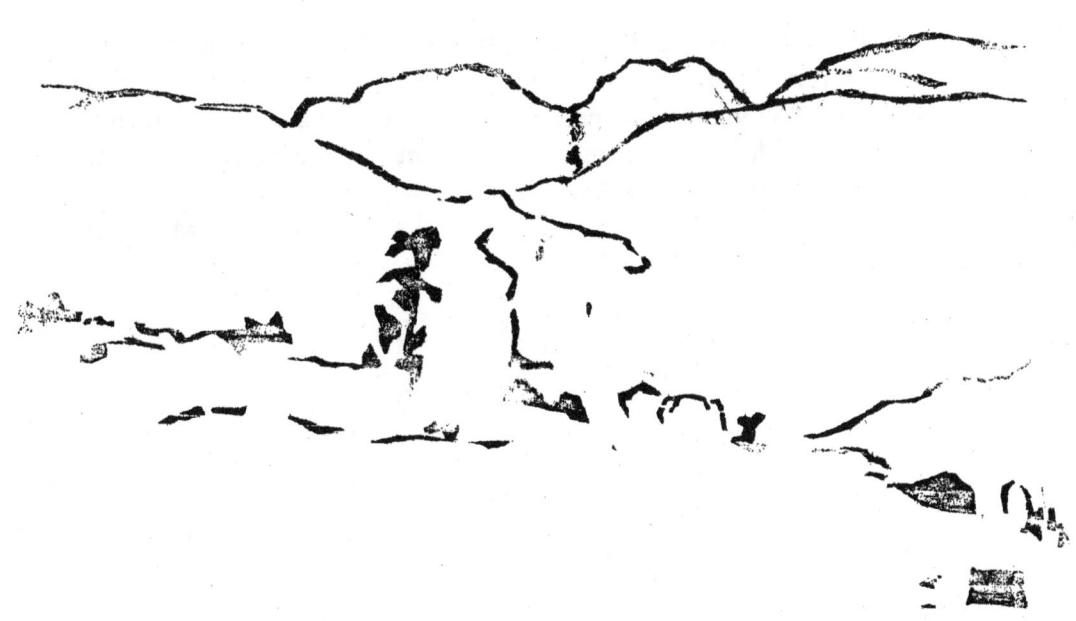

5 Pine tree

It is a strange life, when I consider it, how I endeavor to attain strength and clarity, to mold those base materials into forms which will express me and my attitude, my joy and thankfulness. I work alone, who cares whether I produce anything or not, or who appreciates it? Yet I believe a good thing will not perish.

Journal, April 8, 1963

One of Hubbard's earliest prints.

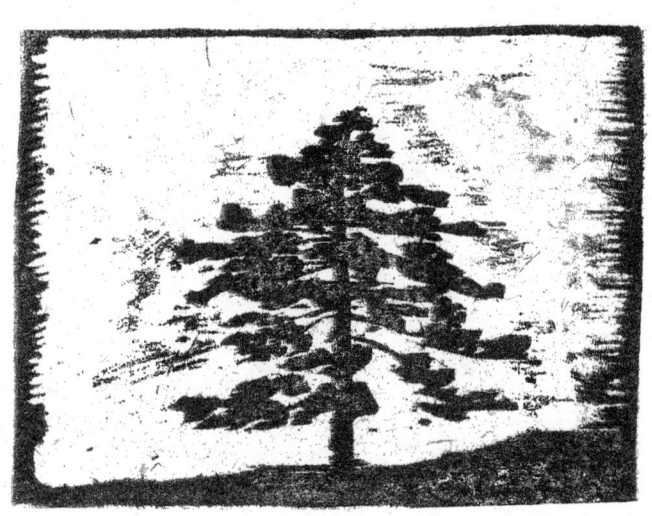

6   Tall plants

On HH list. One of Hubbard's earliest prints.

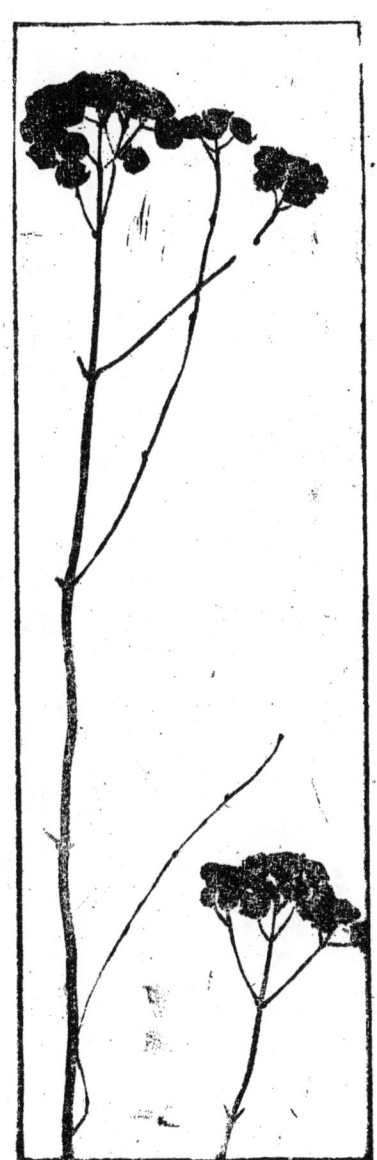

7 Weeds

On HH list. One of Hubbard's earliest prints. Printed in black and gray.

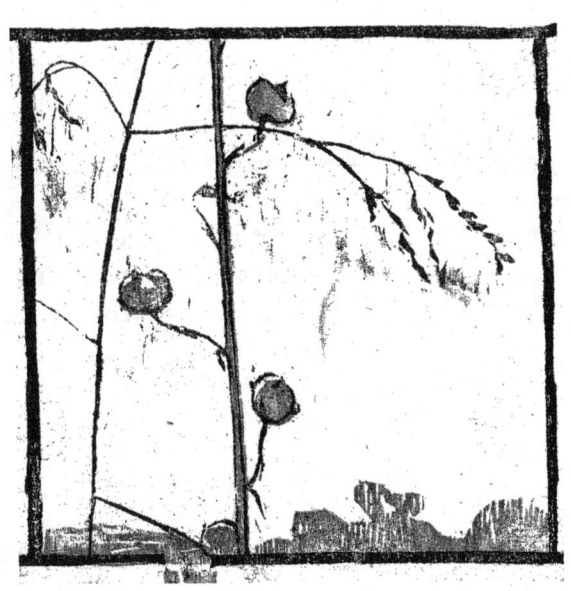

8 Tree trunk with snow

Even through these trivial crowded days, I never lose sight of
the wild earth on which I live, of the ravishing perfection of its
beauty. I stand before infinity and look out over a virgin
wilderness. The potential for reproducing fragments
of this in a form worthy of it are endless.

Journal, January 15, 1987

One star on HH list. Printed in black, gray, and white.

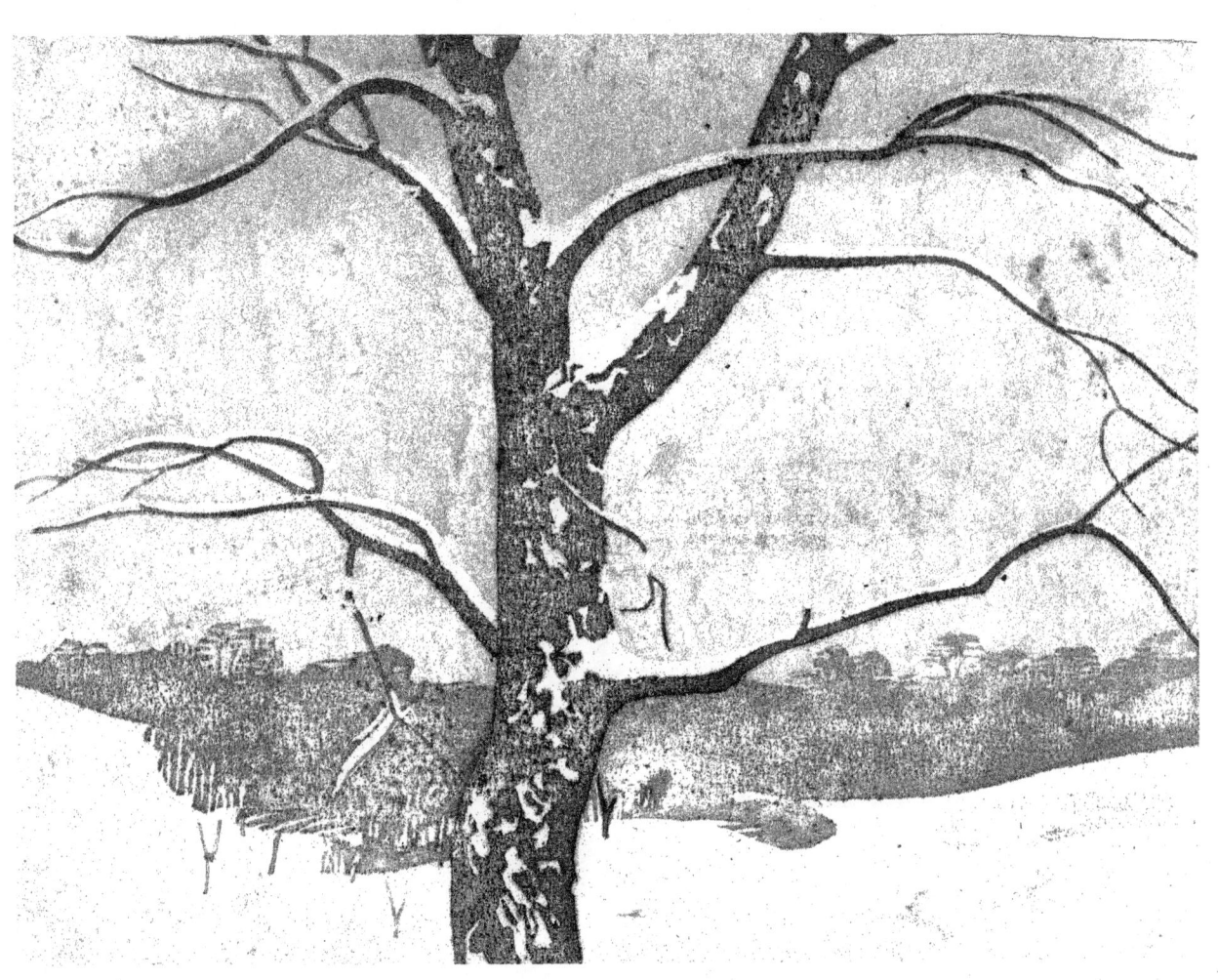

9   Landscape with hills

One of Hubbard's earliest prints.

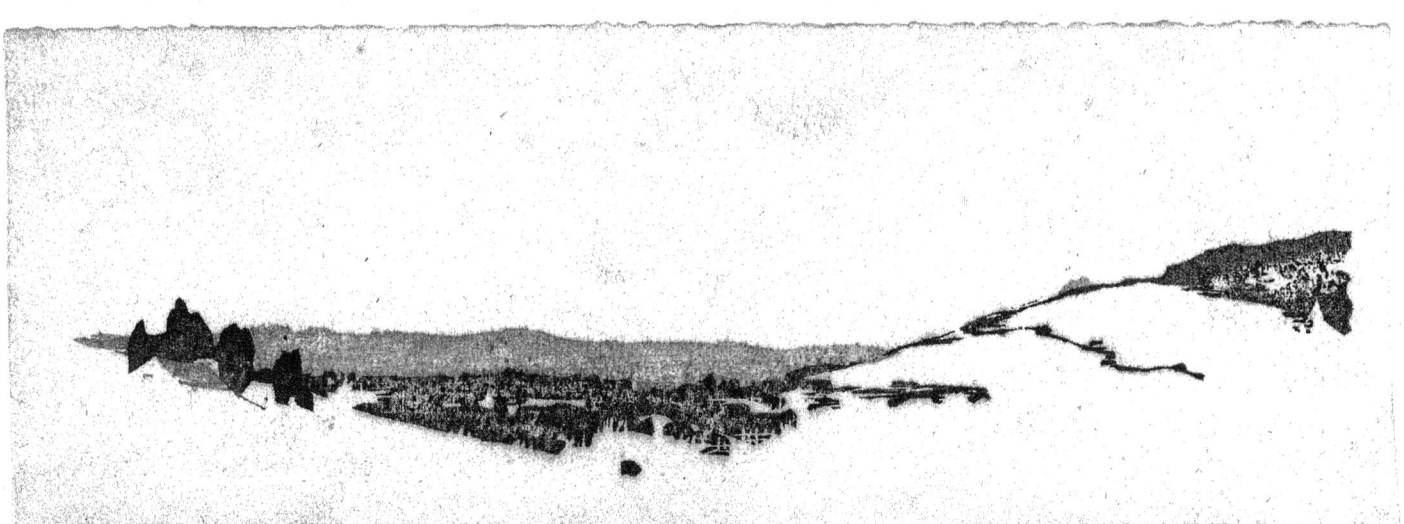

10 Irises

What gives grace to a picture? It is an unconscious
reflection of the grace in the artist's mind.

Journal, June 11, 1964

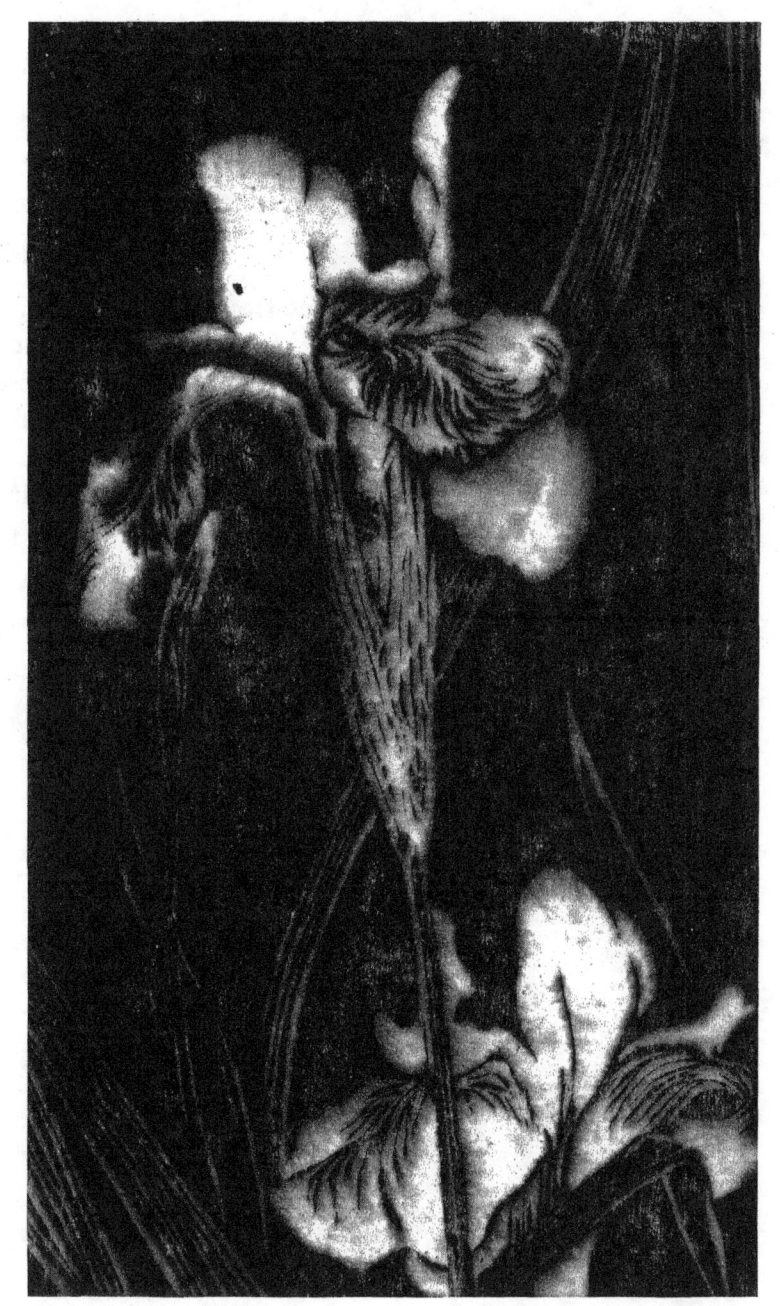

11 Landscape

The impressionists fascinated me from the beginning. But I
had the temerity of youth and I felt that I could go beyond
them and paint landscape in the spirit of Thoreau's observa-
tion of it. I wanted to create a life for myself that would not
mar the earth, but which would be in harmony with it. Here
was everything in one package and I eagerly desired it.

Burdine, *Harlan Hubbard*, page 3

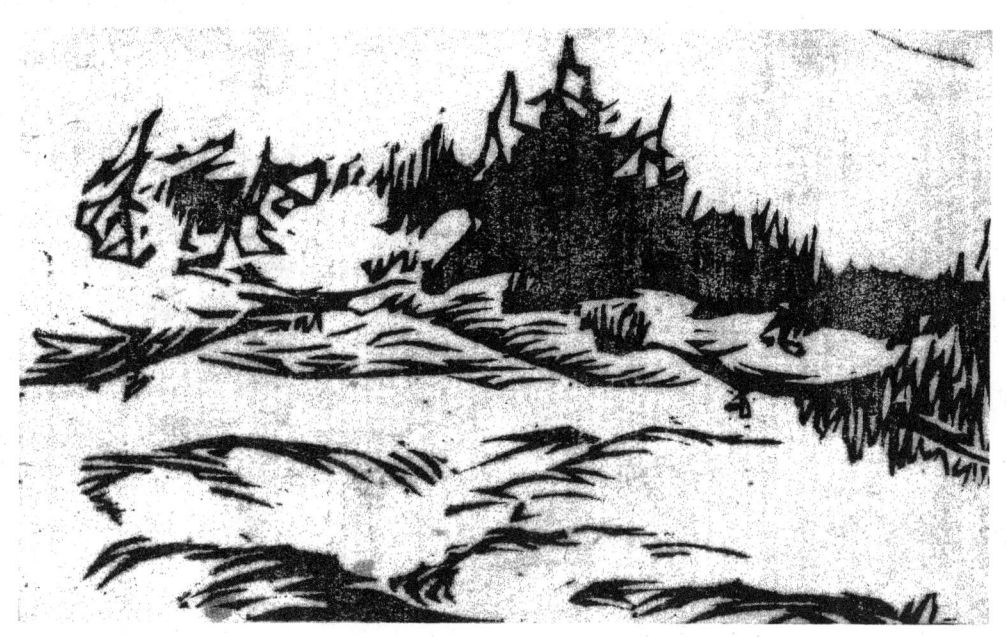

12 River

In this life our attainments fall far short of our desires, even of our capabilities. Yet the joy of a few quiet hours, the sympathy with the outlook and emotions of another (Bach), so close to us over the span of years, the background of the river and hills on this dark wet day—more than a background, it is the foundation, the main theme of my life—the contemplation of it, the resigned waiting, the quiet ecstacy.

Journal, March 12, 1961

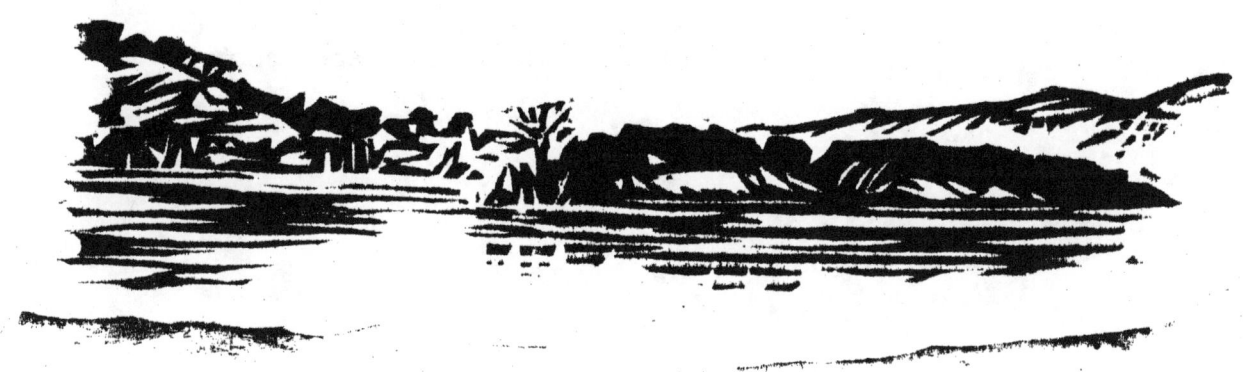

13 River settlement, Stephensport

Hand-labeled "Stephensport" in Hubbard's collection.

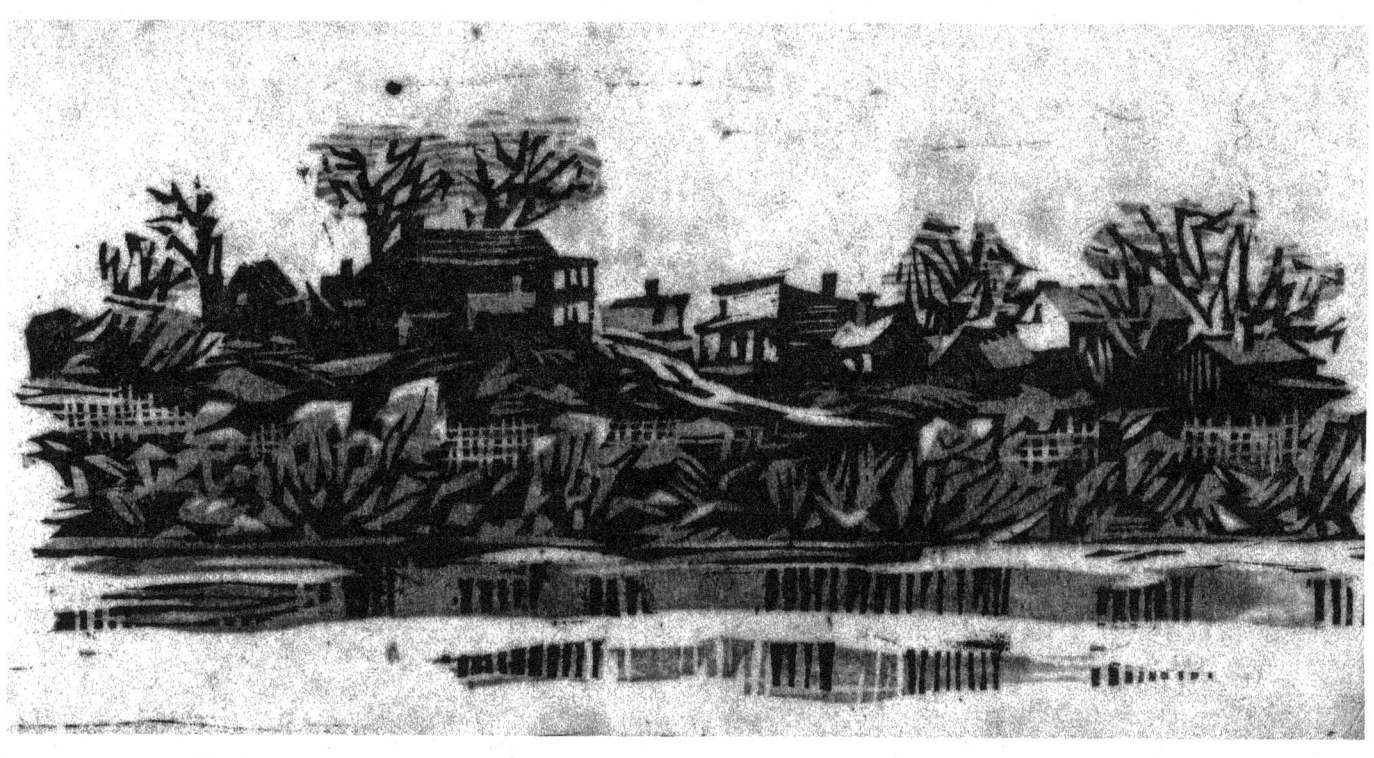

14   Houses in winter

Printed in black and gray. Hand signed in pencil.

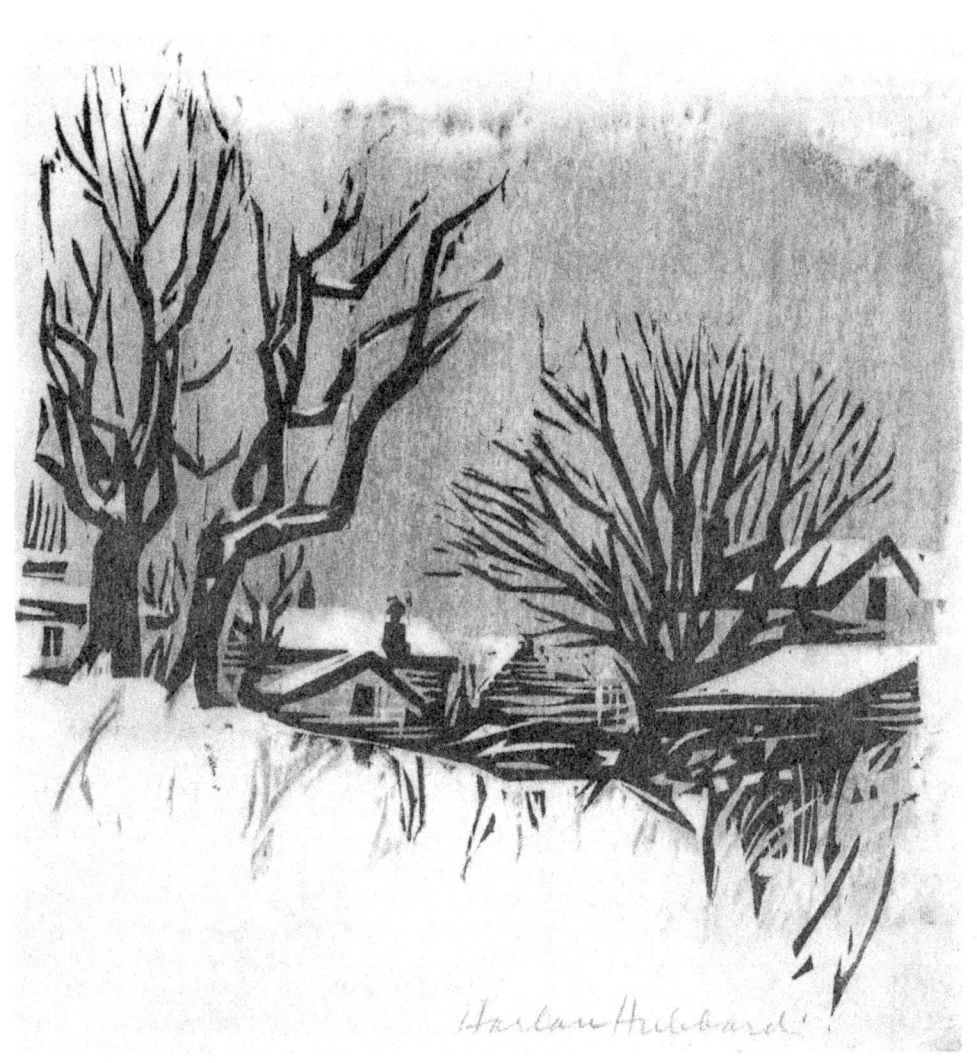

Harlan Hubbard

15   Farmhouse

Two stars on HH list.

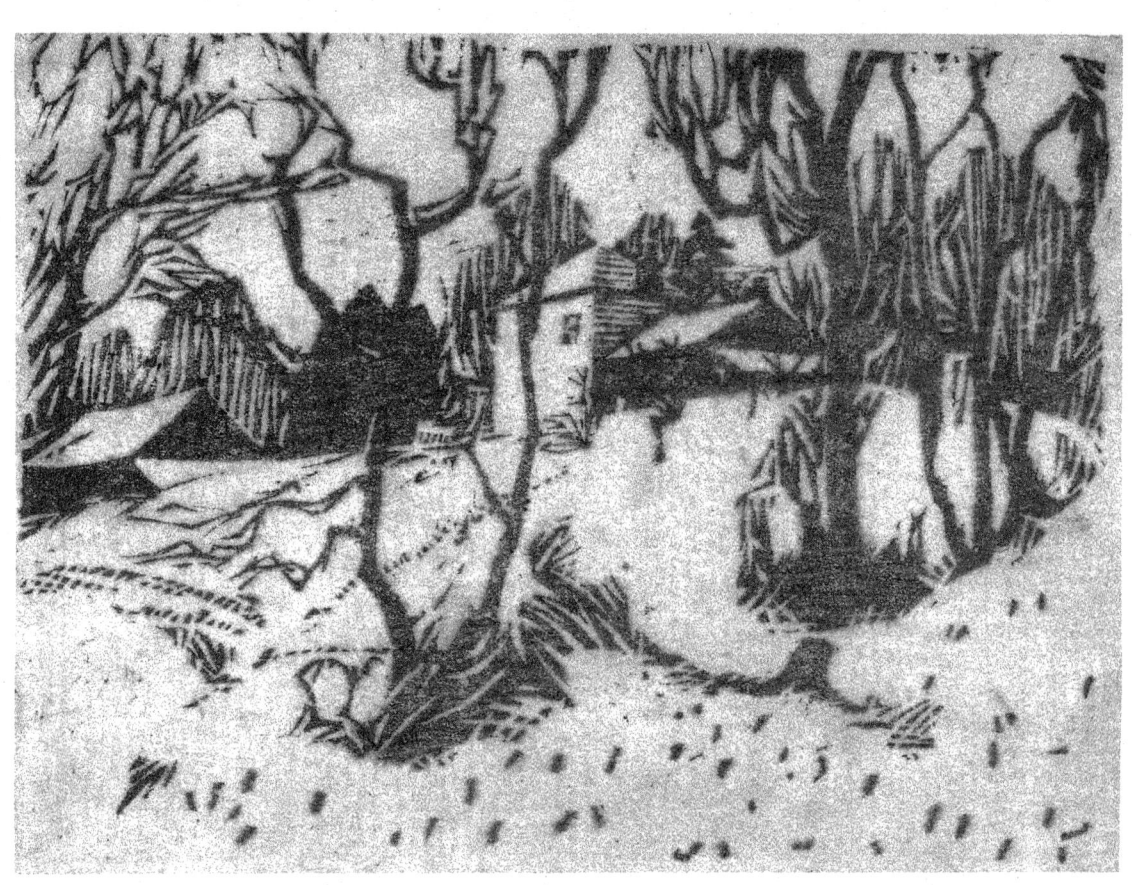

16 Rocky hillside

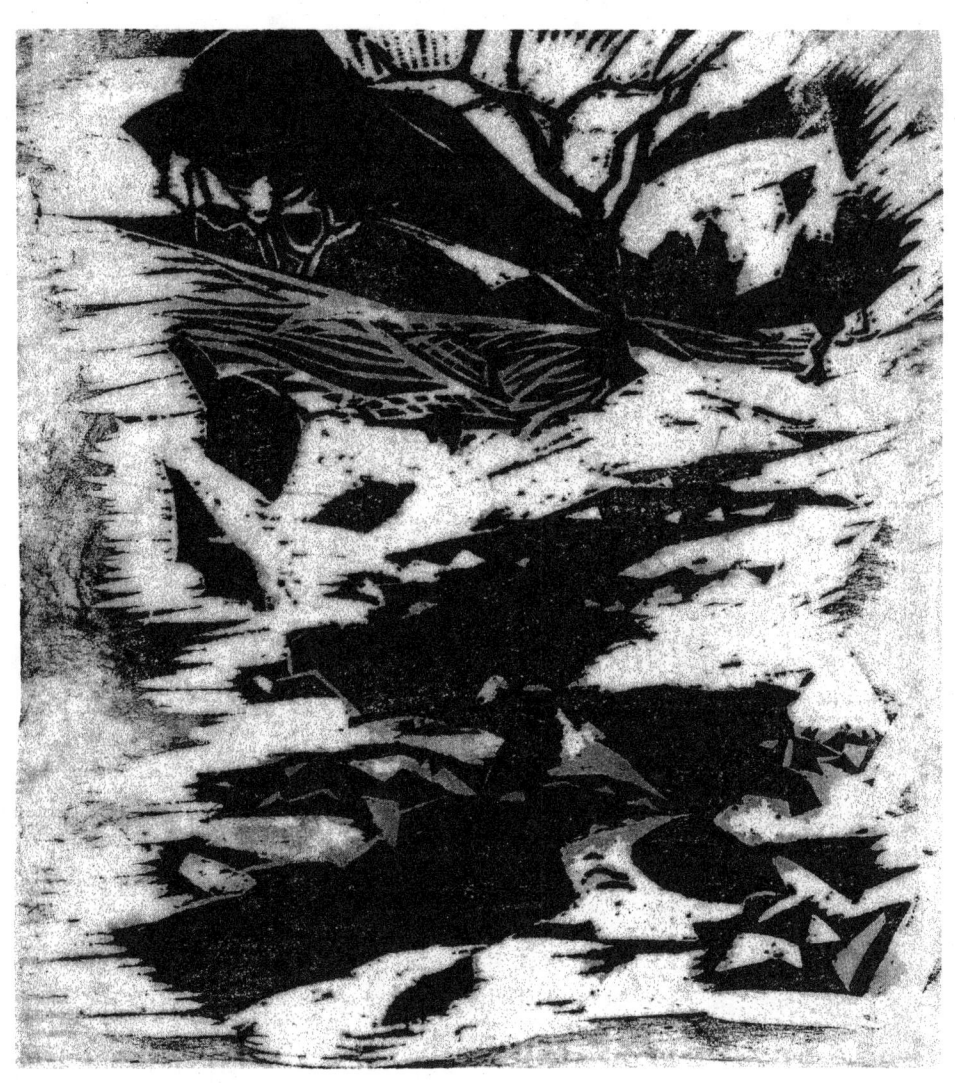

17   Winter farmstead, Northern Kentucky

Two stars on HH list.

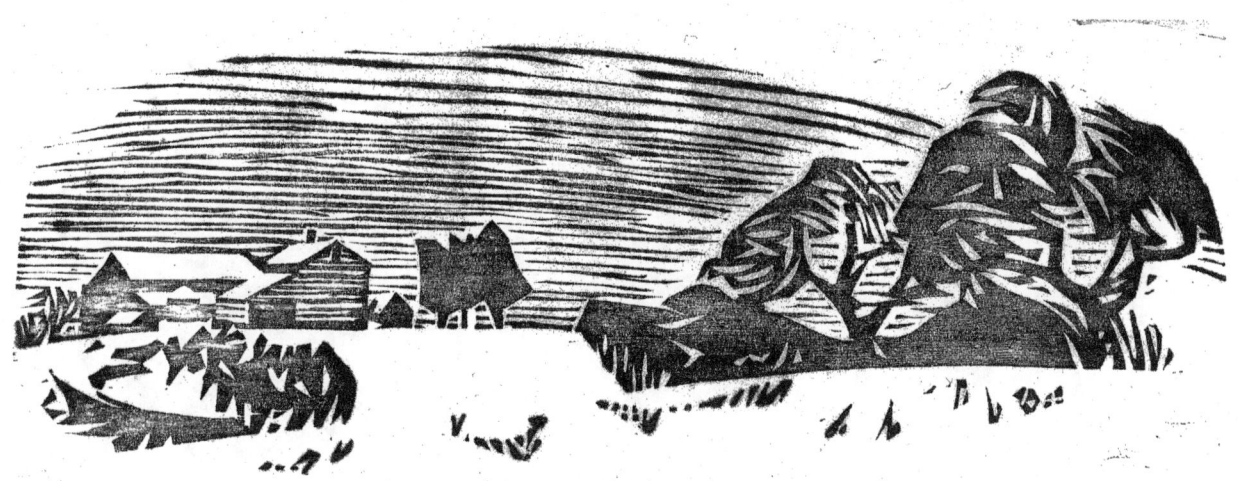

18   Farmhouse, June 1935

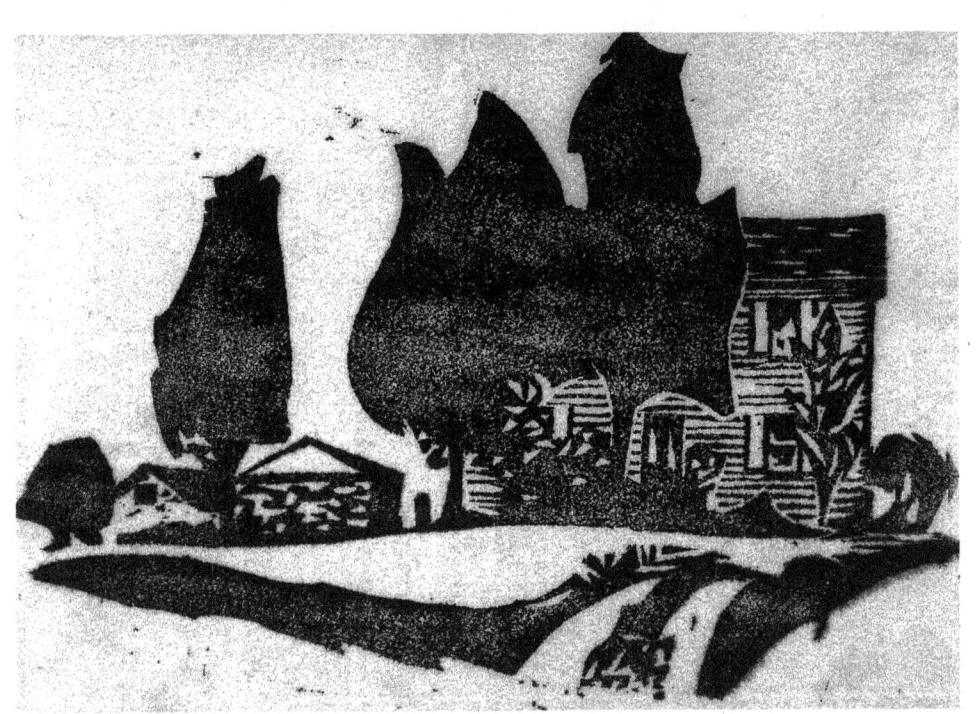

19 River town

My grandiose ideas of life and art had to wait. But the flame did
not burn out. In the meantime, I rediscovered the Ohio River.
Now I became conscious of its unique beauty and interest.
It seemed to deserve a whole school of painters. And my
ambition was to live and work within its boundaries.

Interview with Florence Fowler Burdine

Printed in black and two shades of gray.
Original dimensions: 8" x 5 1/2".

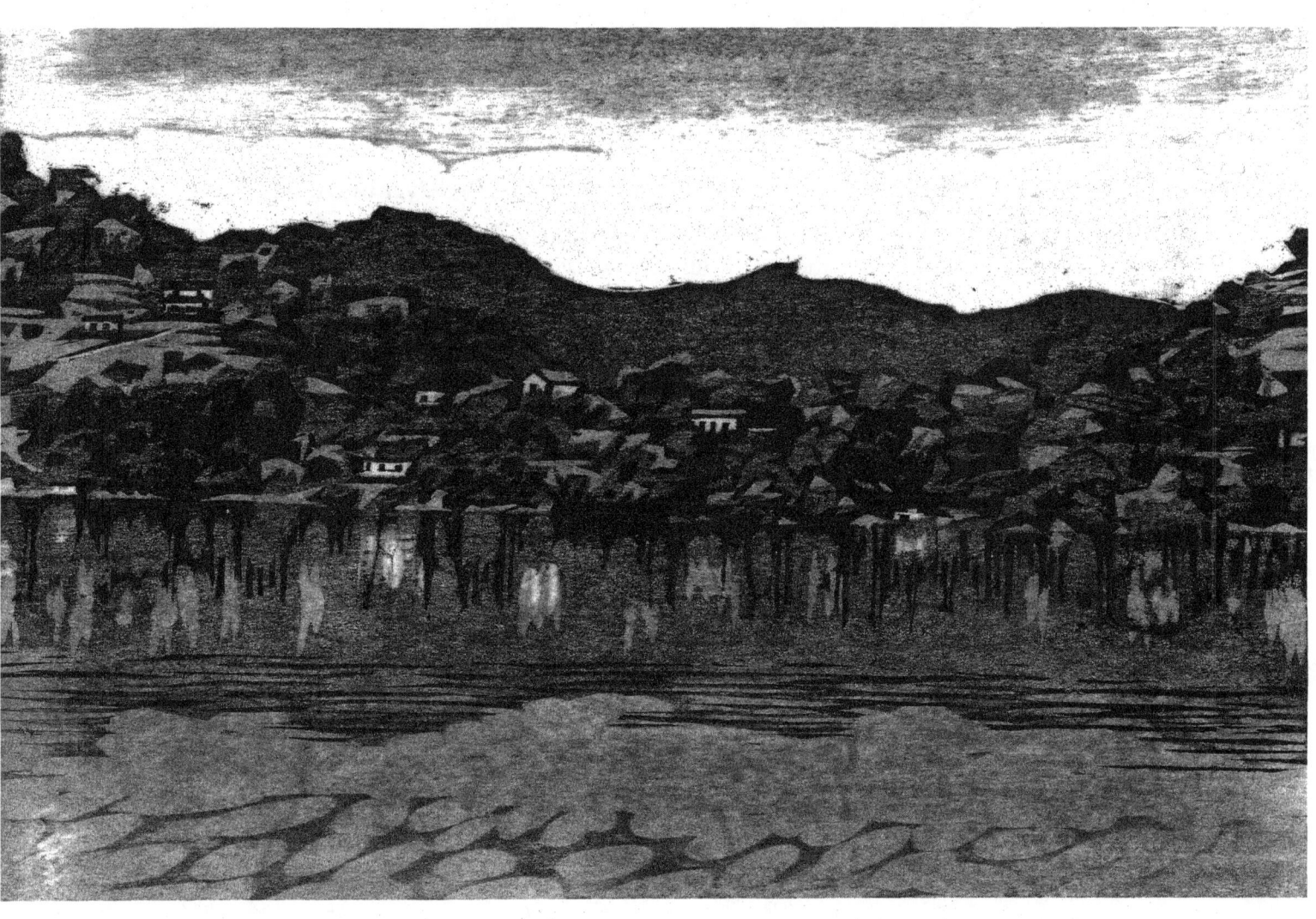

20   River in winter

The river in the sun yesterday, reflecting the blue sky,
the sunny hills in their winter warmth and bareness.
Later under the cloudy sky the reflections of the
dark hills were blue and purple.

Journal, November 29, 1962

One star on HH list.

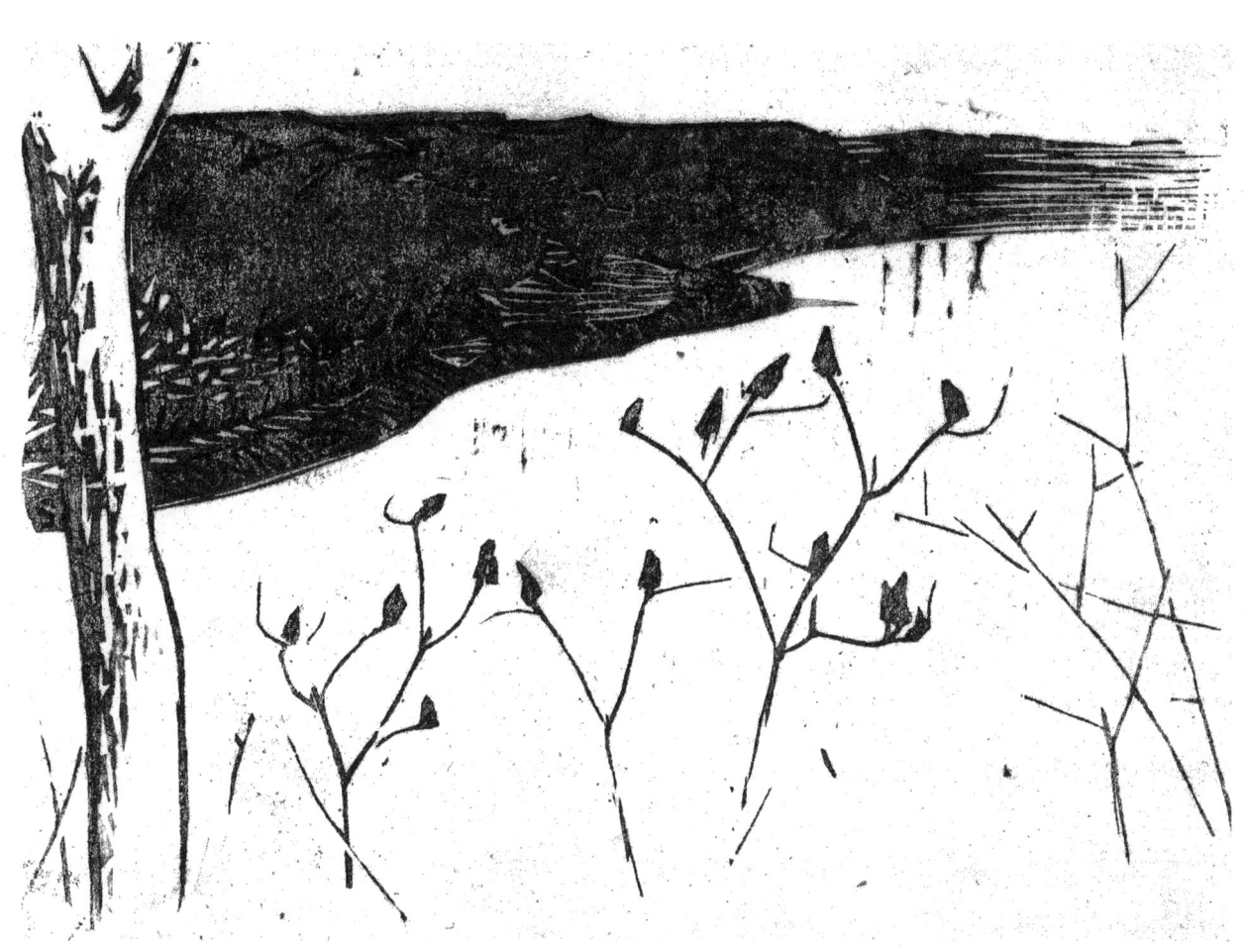

21 Shantyboats at Brent, Kentucky

A river traveler might pass by without noticing it. There was not a
steeple or a smokestack to mark a town, and the shantyboats were
scattered along half a mile of shore, often hidden in the willows.

Journals, 1929-1944, page 42

Printed in black and pale reddish brown.
Original dimensions: 8 ½" x 5 ⅞".

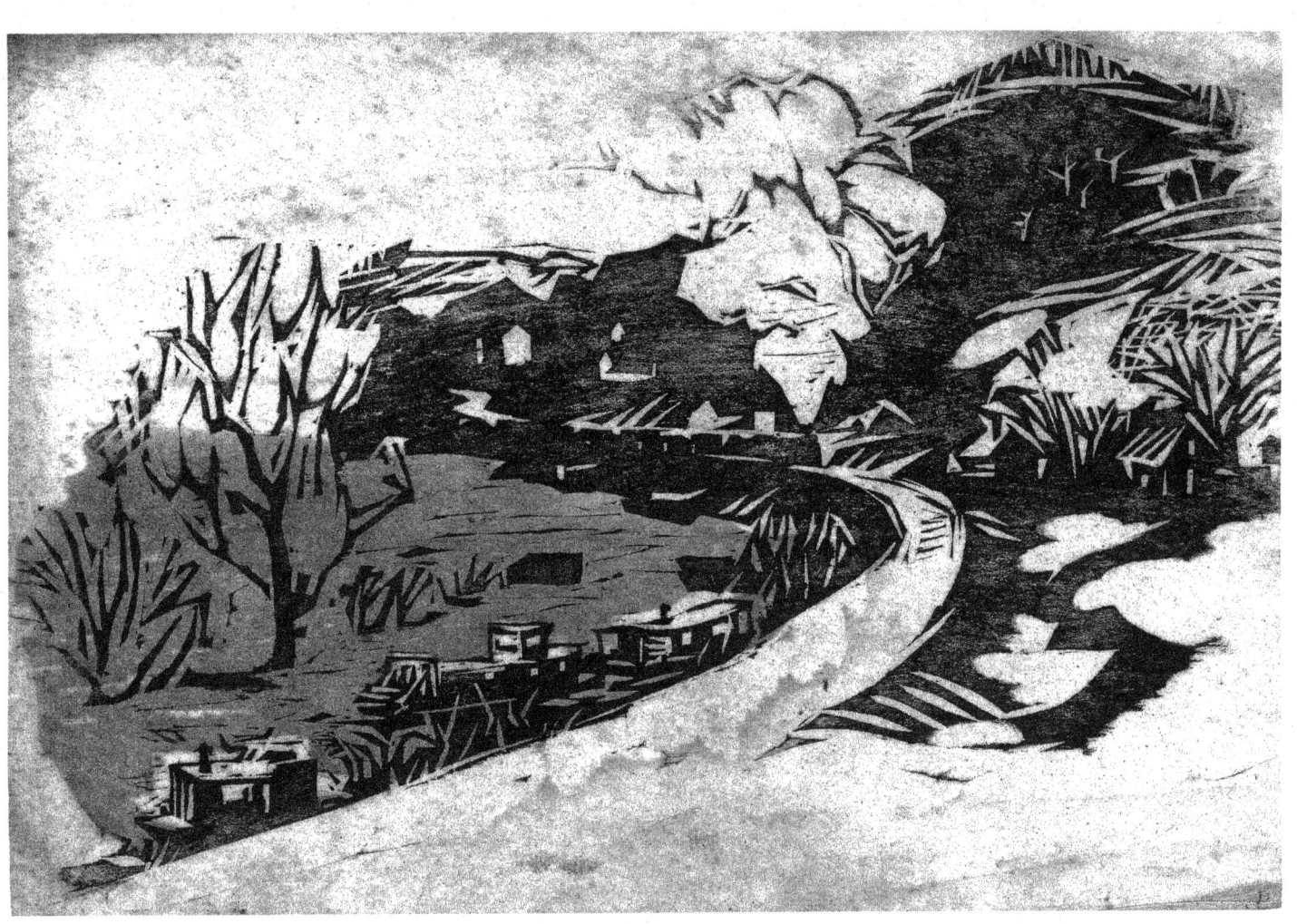

22 Steamboat

It might have been the steamboats which drew my attention up the
river. They passed upstream in the evening, bound for legendary
places—Pomeroy, Charleston, Gallipolis, and Point Pleasant. Downstream they ran only to Cincinnati, which was then the end of the river
to me. These boats could not be compared with the grand steamboats of
the golden age. Though old and shabby, and fallen into unprosperous
days, these last survivors of a proud tradition had about them a
dignity and grace which are gone from today's river.

Shantyboat, page 83

Printed by Hubbard in black only; in black and gray; in black and pink; and in black,
gray, and a very light pink or peach. The version in black and gray is reproduced here.

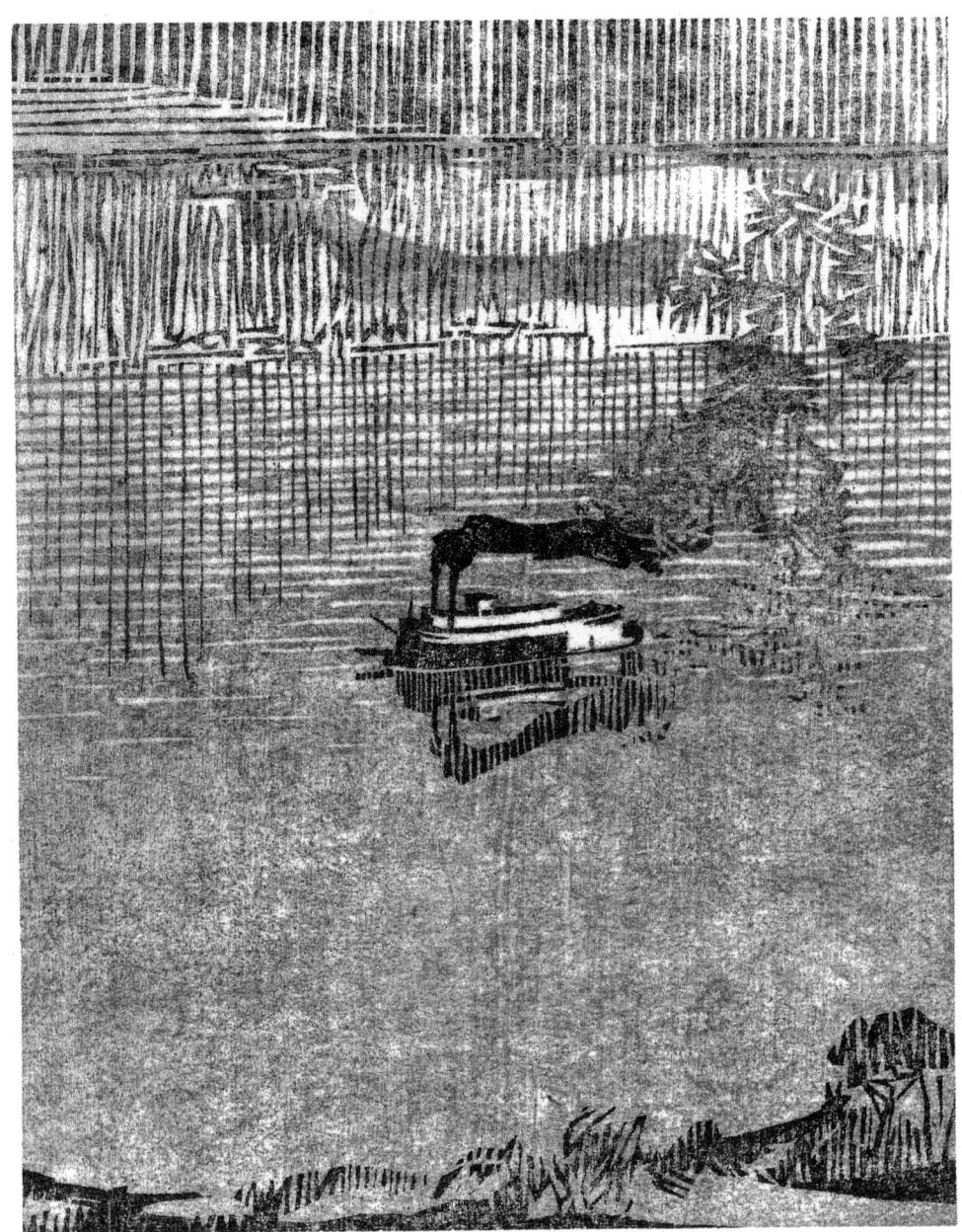

23 Winter landscape

The cold returns like an old friend. He is rough and unmanageable, but he brings many pleasures with him, like fires and wood-cutting. He simplifies and contracts our living, our circle of activity is more confined. Yet winter opens our outlook to its widest. It gives us energy and courage to take on again the high endeavors we have shirked through the sultry heat of summer.

Journal, October 23, 1962

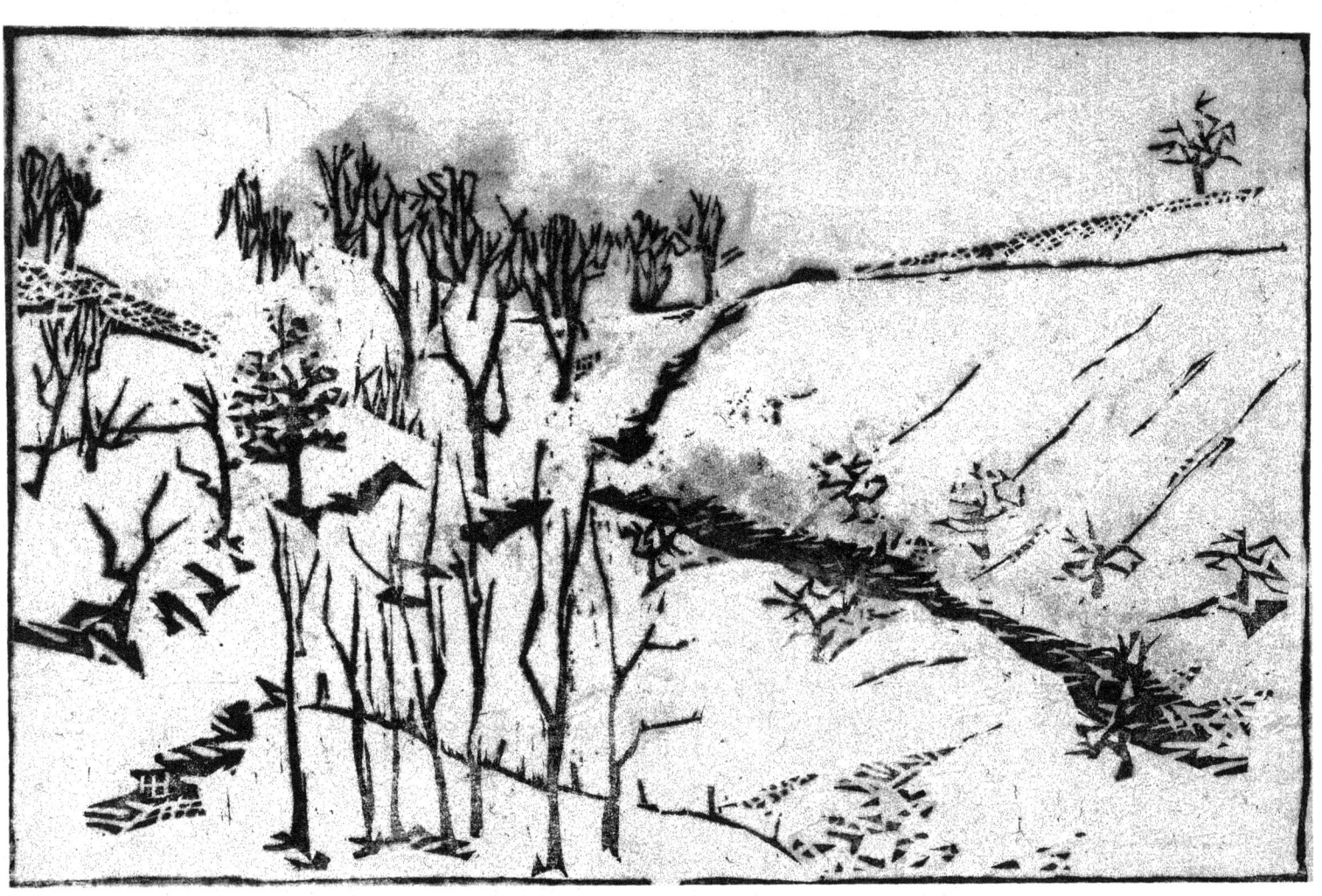

24   Farmhouse

One star on HH list. Printed in black and gray.

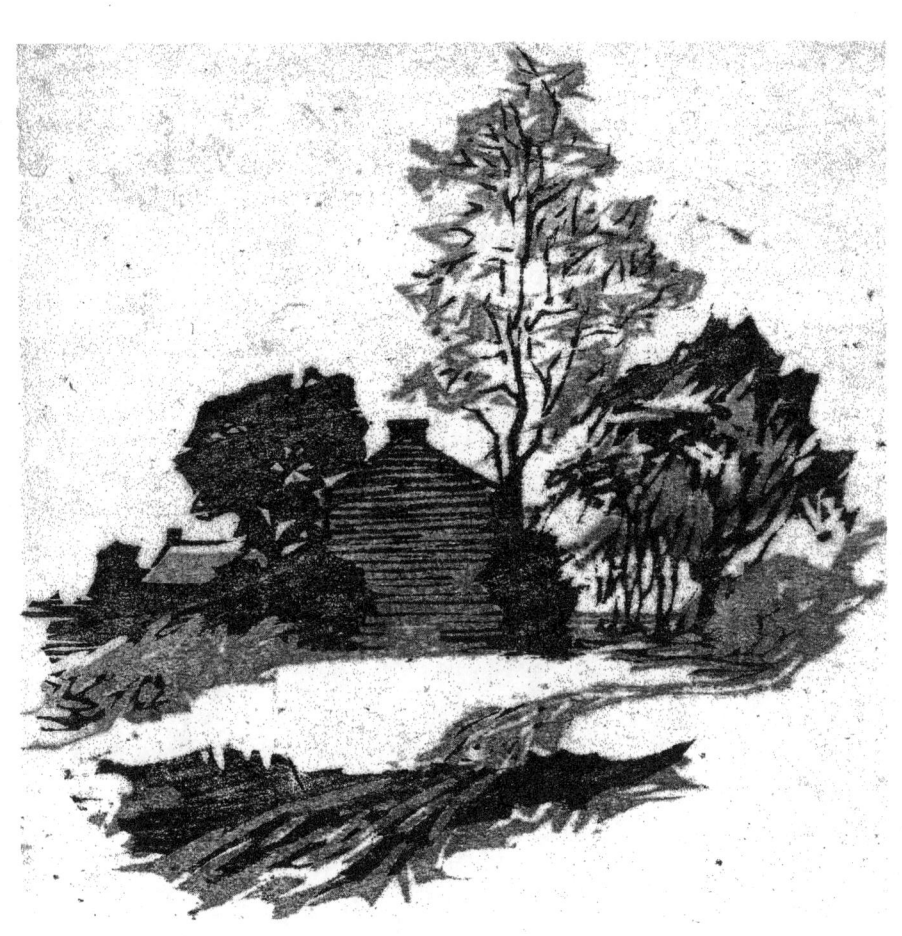

25 Campbell County farmhouse

The chok chok of an axe, on a winter evening, the sun having set
over the snowy earth, the new moon beginning to shine. Man has
evolved into this social, technological, intellectual animal, but
perhaps another development is possible, in another direction.
He need not modify and subdue the earth, his home, nor
forget that he is a part of the natural system.

Journal, January 26, 1966

Two stars on HH list. Printed in black and gray.

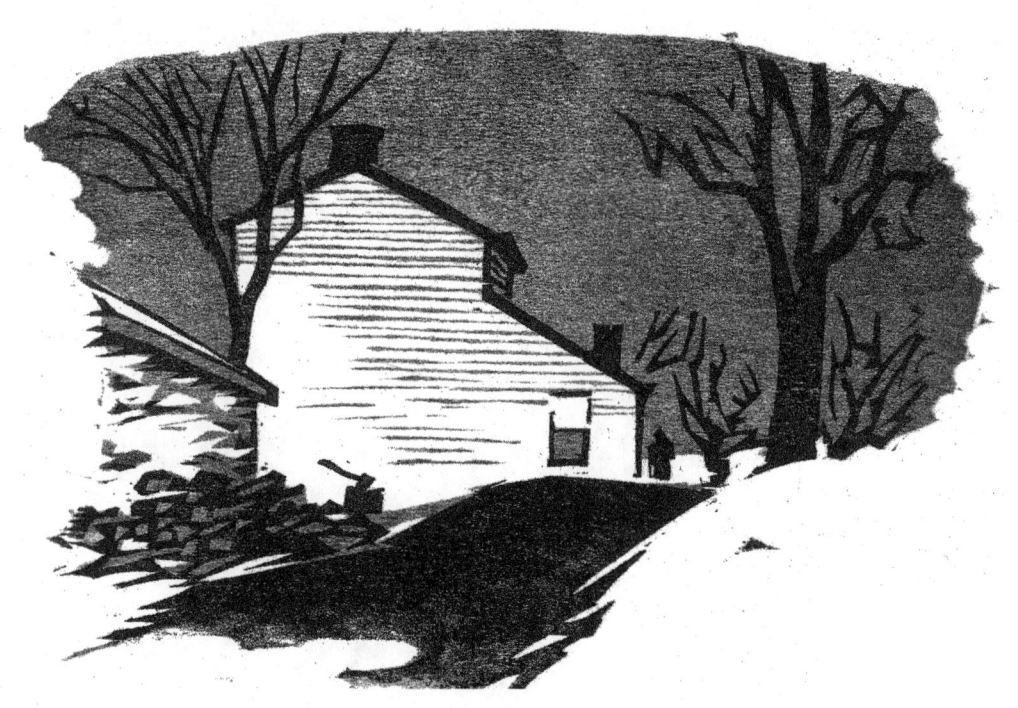

26 Aurora, Indiana

On HH list. Original dimensions: 11 $^{15}\!/_{16}$" x 5 $^{15}\!/_{16}$".

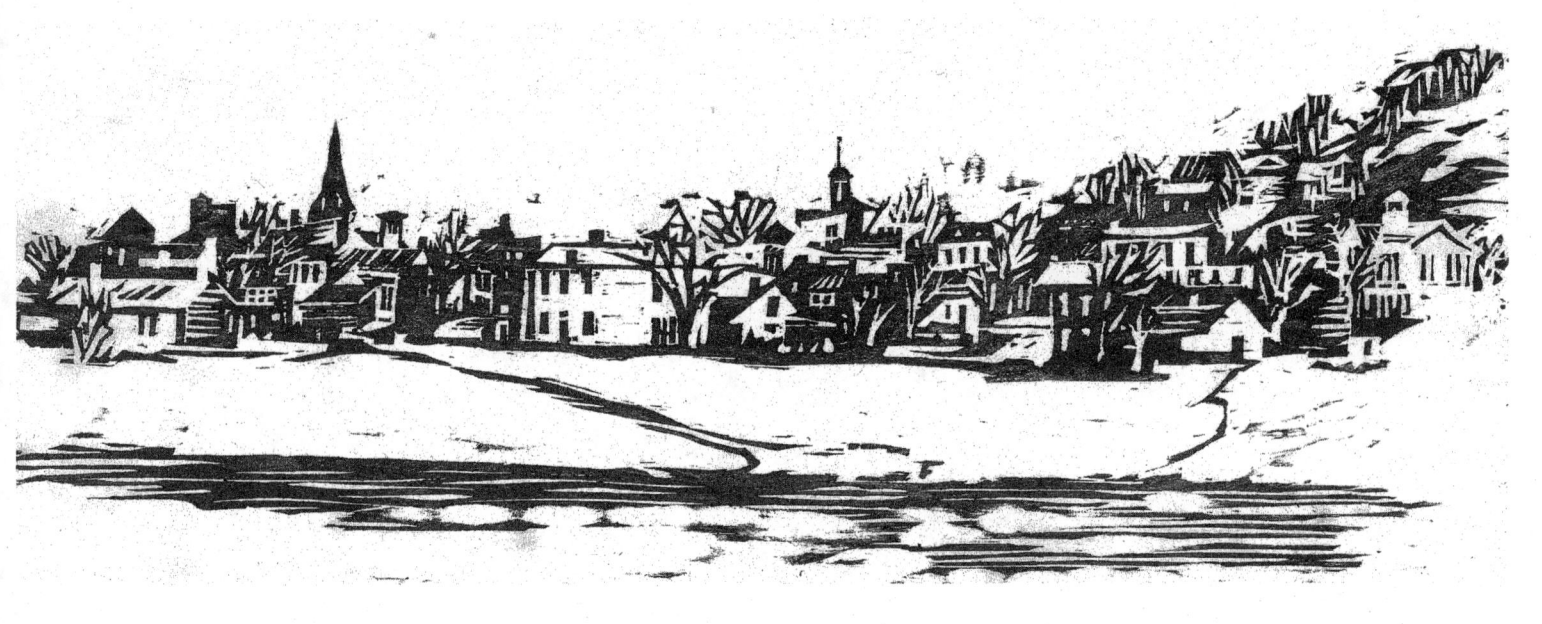

27 Harper's Ferry, West Virginia

One star on HH list. Printed in black and gray.
Original dimensions: 8 ⅛" x 5 ½".

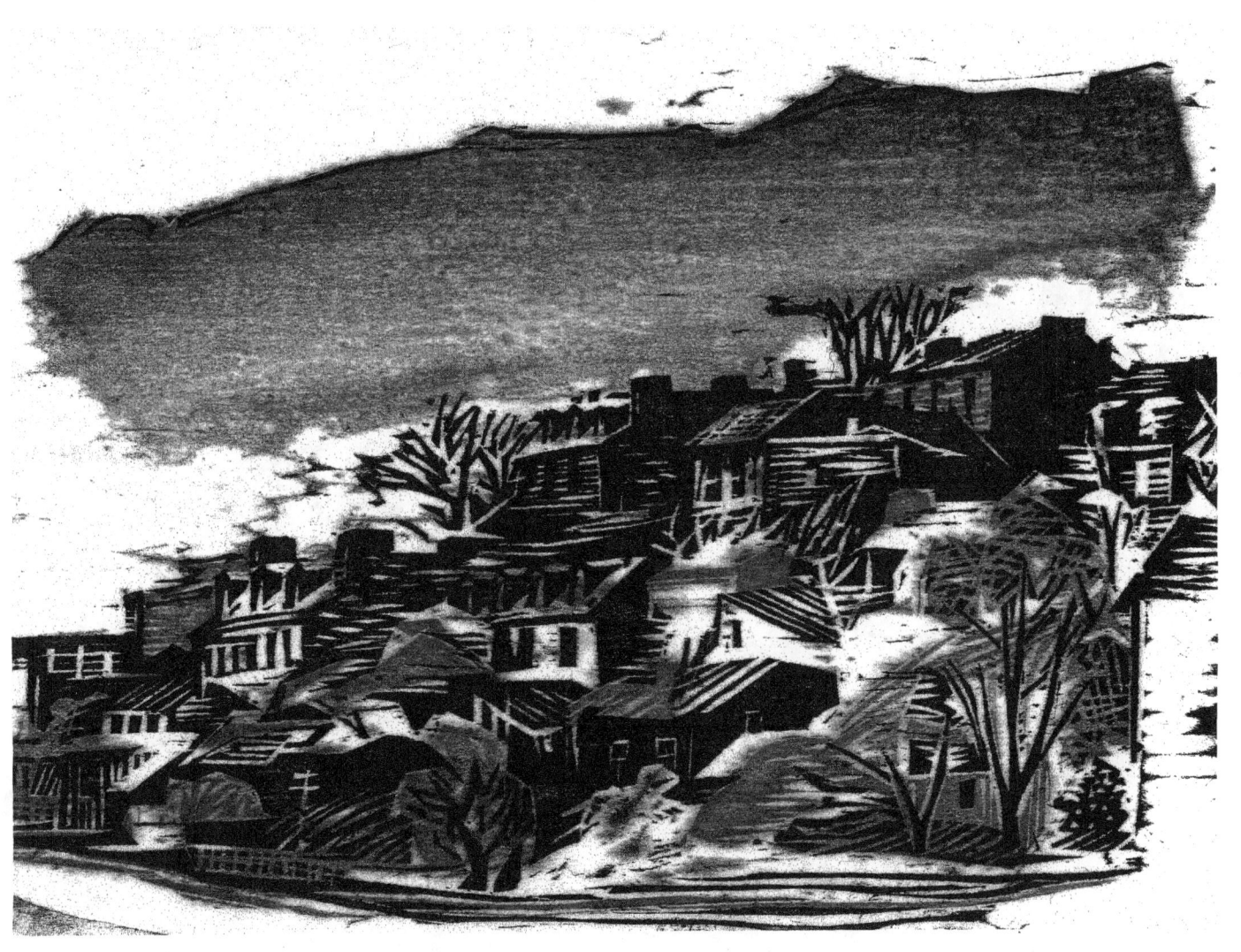

28 Summer landscape

This continued fair, warm weather, and the ripening of the earth,
from green summer to the varied and brilliant colors of autumn,
affords a glimpse of life on a higher level than we know. It is
marvelous that our daily lives go on amid this splendor.

Journal, October 17, 1963

Original dimensions: 11 ¾" x 5 ¹¹⁄₁₆".

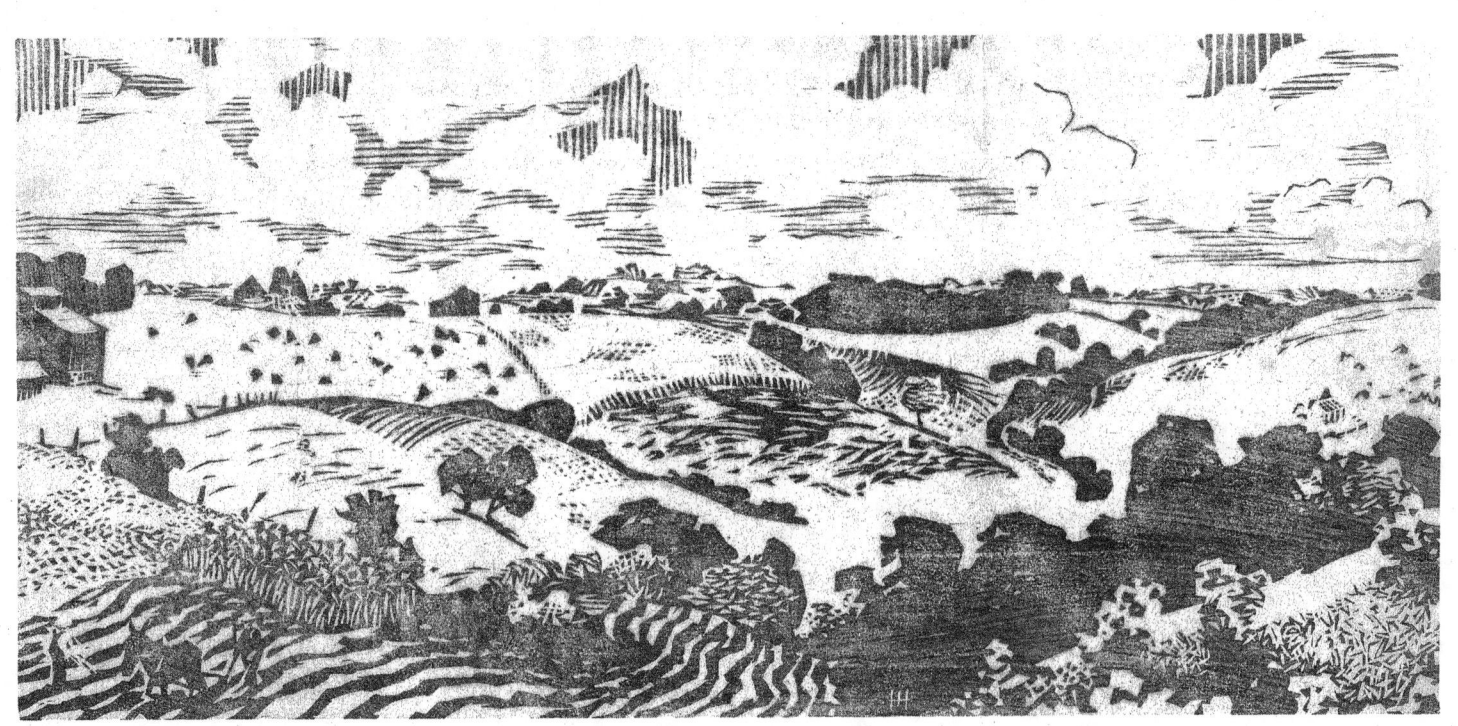

29 Ohio River

With me, the attraction of flowing water goes back as far
as I can remember. My river is the Ohio, whose channel
from the first has borne the dreams of men from the old
and known to the new and strange.

Shantyboat, page 1

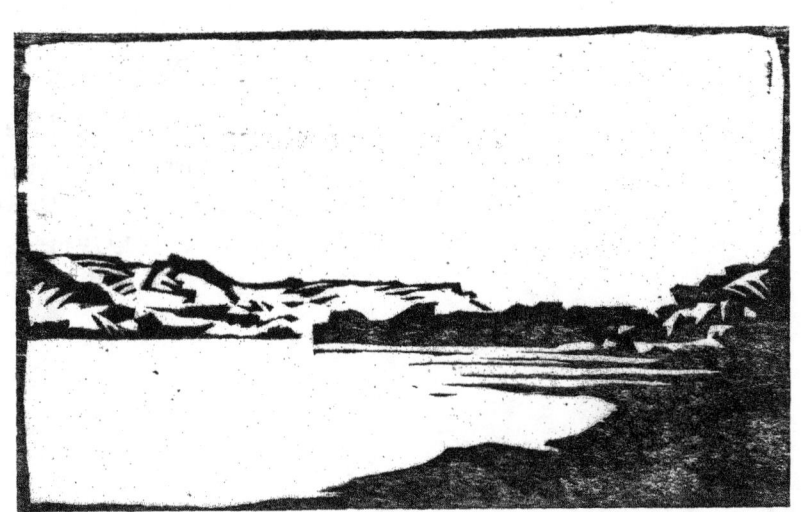

30 Ohio River packet

I look back on the bygone steamboats with love and
longing. A large part of my artistic effort has gone
toward expressing my gratitude to them.

Journals, 1929-1944, page 51

Two stars on HH list.

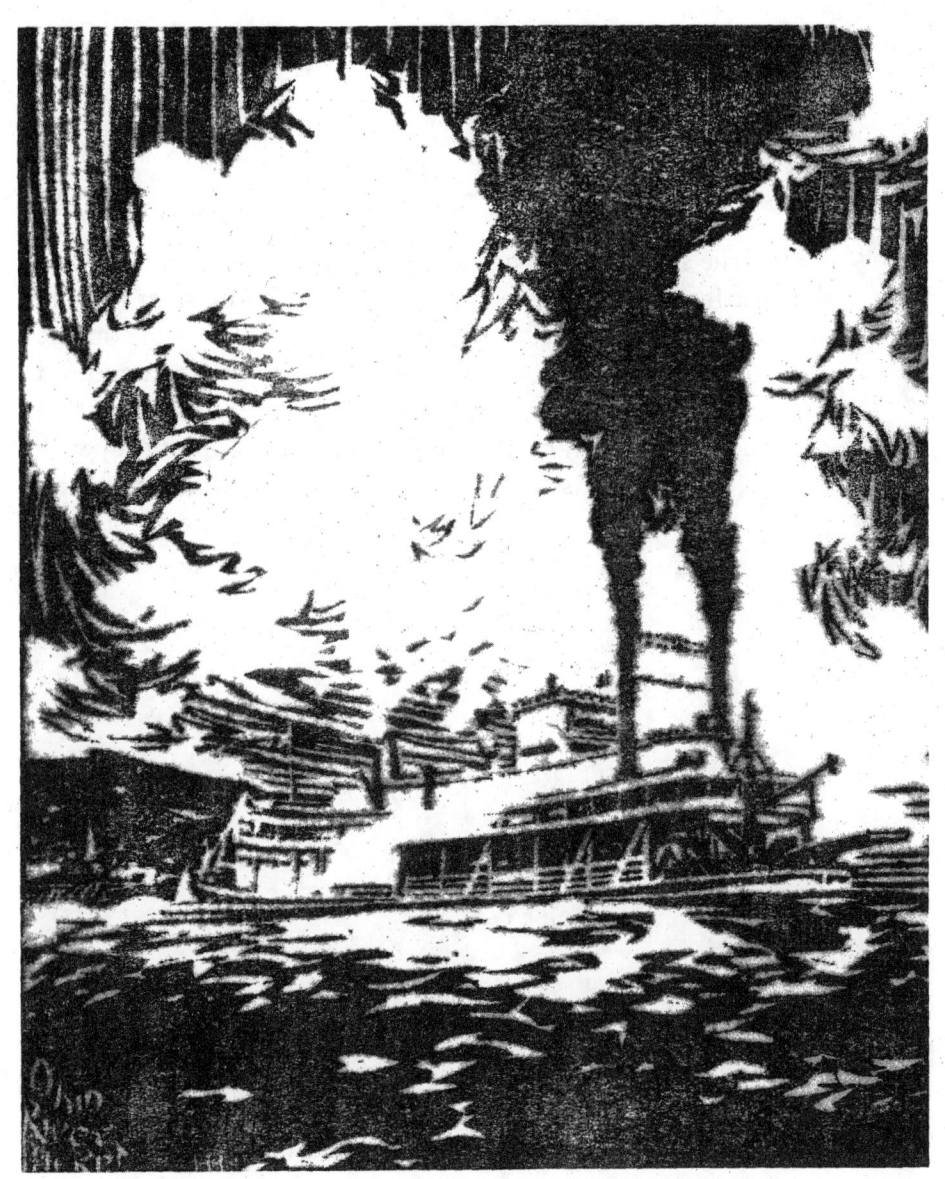

31 Shantyboater pulling a skiff

The true shantyboater has a purer love for the river than had
his drifting flatboat predecessors. . . . To him the river is more
than a means of livelihood. It is a way of life, the only one he
knows which answers his innate longing to be untrammeled
and independent, to live on the fringe of society, almost
beyond the law, beyond taxes and ownership of property.
His drifting downstream is as natural to him
as his growing old in the stream of time.

Shantyboat, page 3

Printed in black, with highlights in white ink.

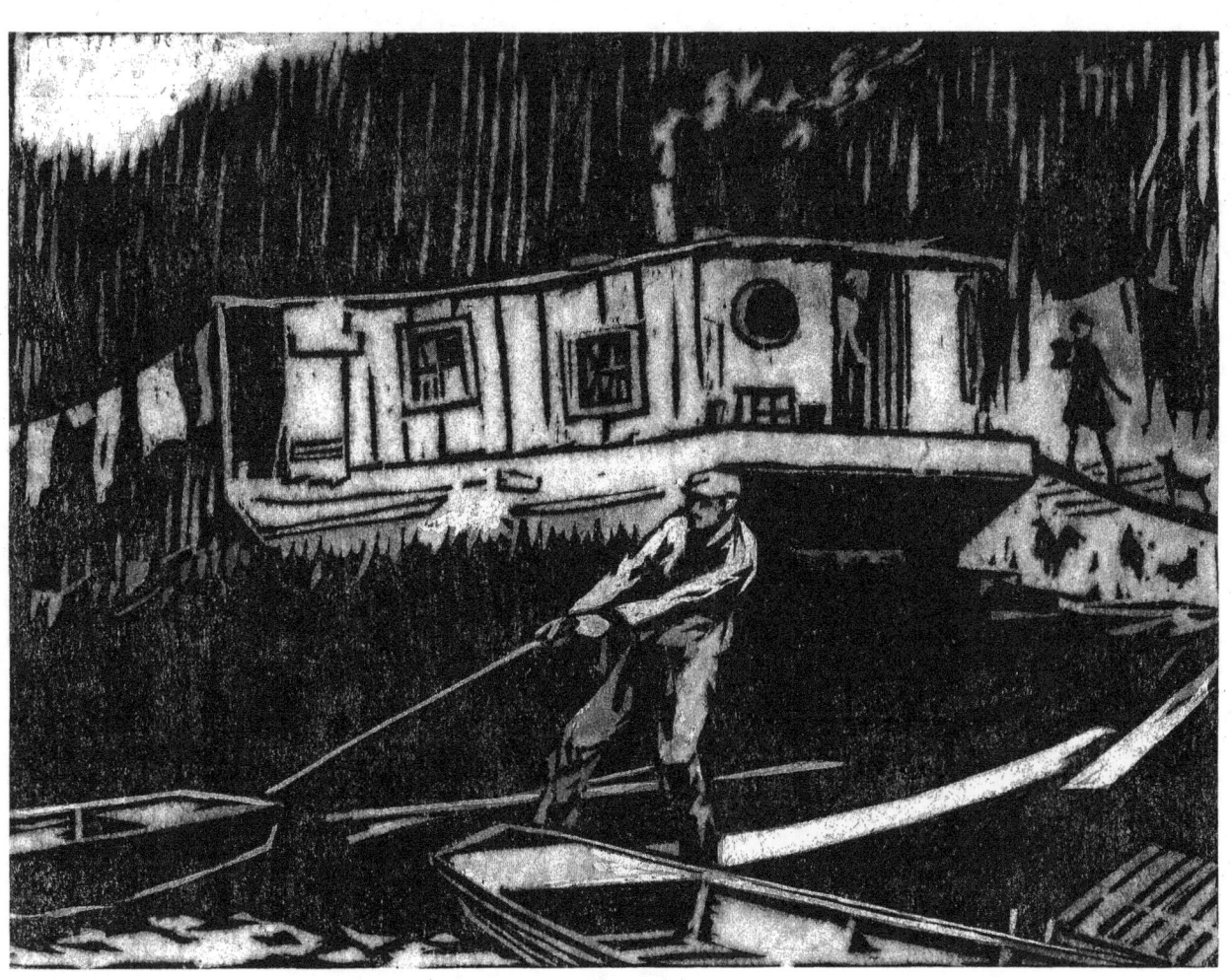

32   Shantyboat on a bank

Brent had always been a haven for shantyboats and a sizable remnant of the colony remained. Most of the small boats were beached out on the steep bank at different levels. A large house-boat lay a little way downstream where the bank was less steep; it was there, and the same family lived on it, twenty years later when I was building my own shantyboat nearby.

Journals, 1929-1944, page 3

Printed by Konrad Juestel.

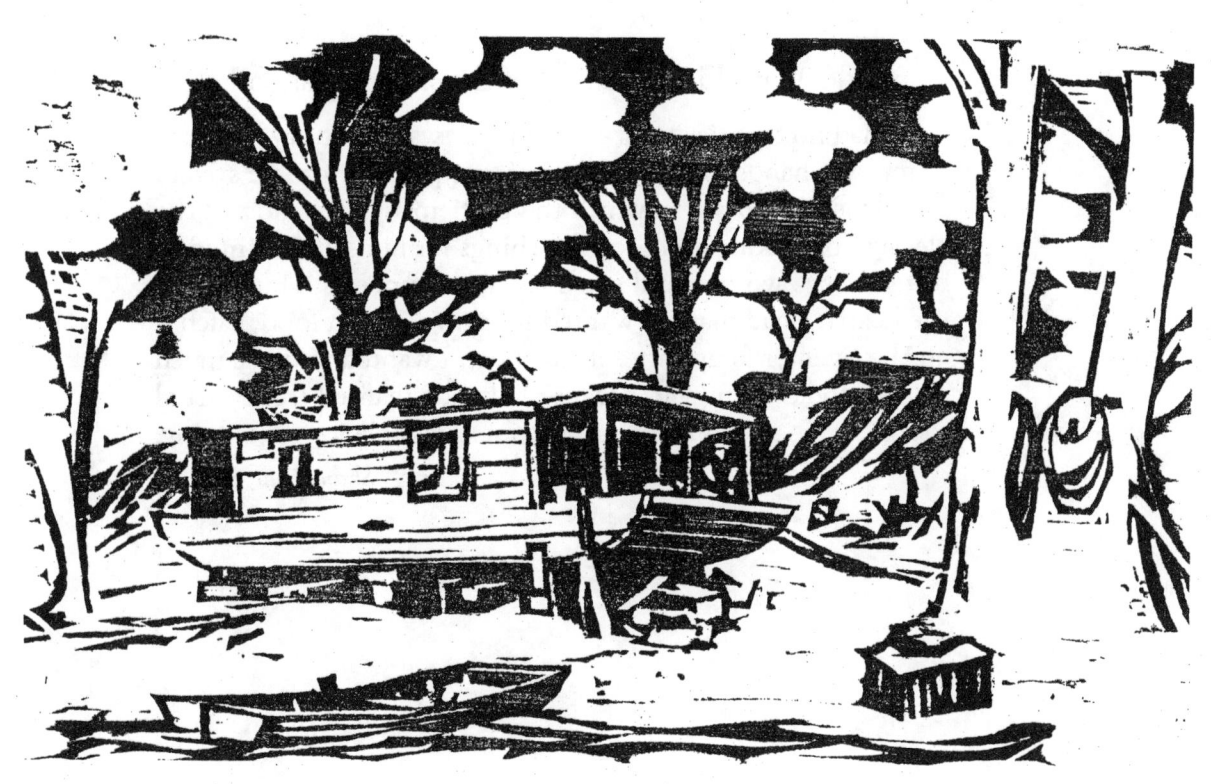

33 Building the hull of the shantyboat, fall 1944

I had no theories to prove. I merely wanted to try living by
my own hands, independent as far as possible from a system
of division of labor in which the participant loses most of the
pleasure of making and growing things for himself. I wanted to
bring in my own fuel and smell its sweet smoke as it burned on
the hearth I had made. I wanted to grow my own food, catch it
in the river, or forage after it. In short, I wanted to do as much
as I could for myself, because I already realized from partial
experience the inexpressible joy of so doing.

Shantyboat, page 38

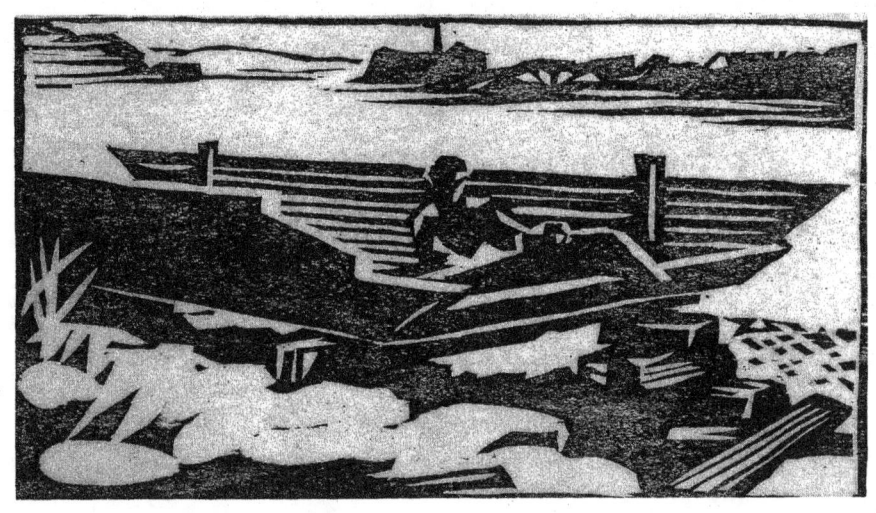

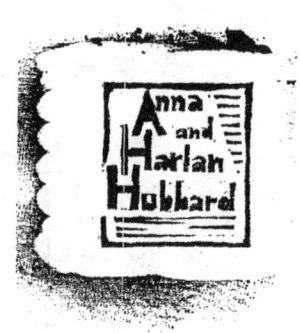

34 Stamp

The smallest of Hubbard's known prints.

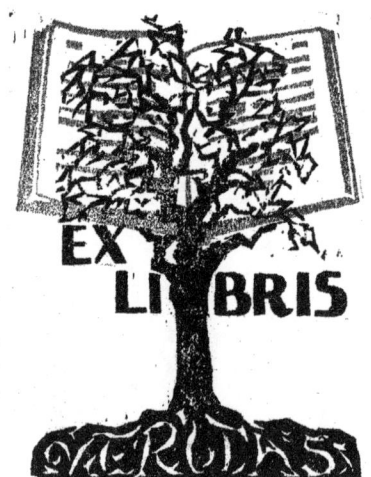

35 Bookplate, "Ex Libris, Veritas"

Printed in black and brown.

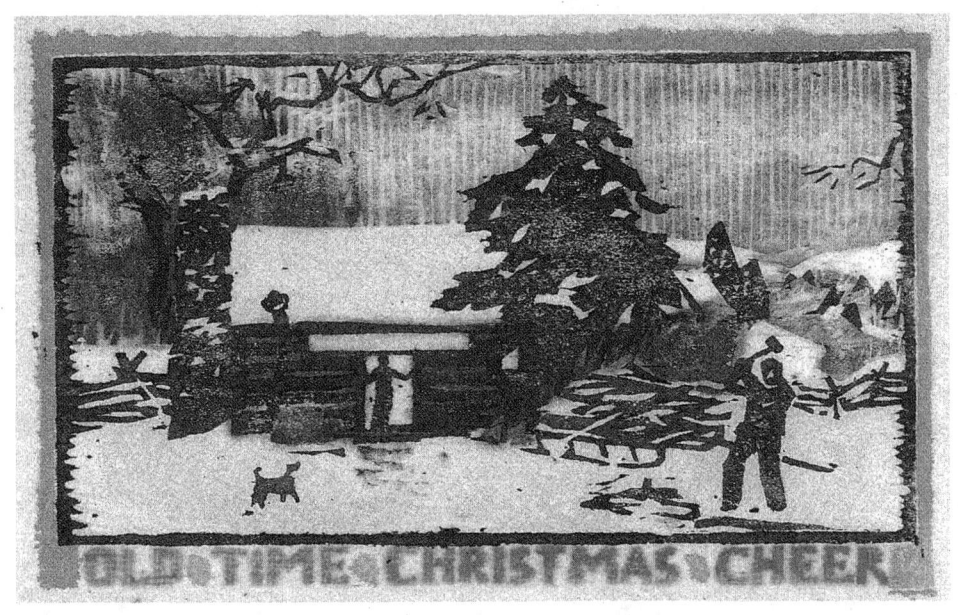

OLD TIME CHRISTMAS CHEER

I Cabin

When in high school, I stumbled onto a book of Thoreau's
Walden. This aroused a desire in me to go into the woods
myself, build a cabin and live close to the earth.

Interview with John Morgan

Ca. 1924. One of Hubbard's earliest woodcuts.
White ink on snow-covered areas.

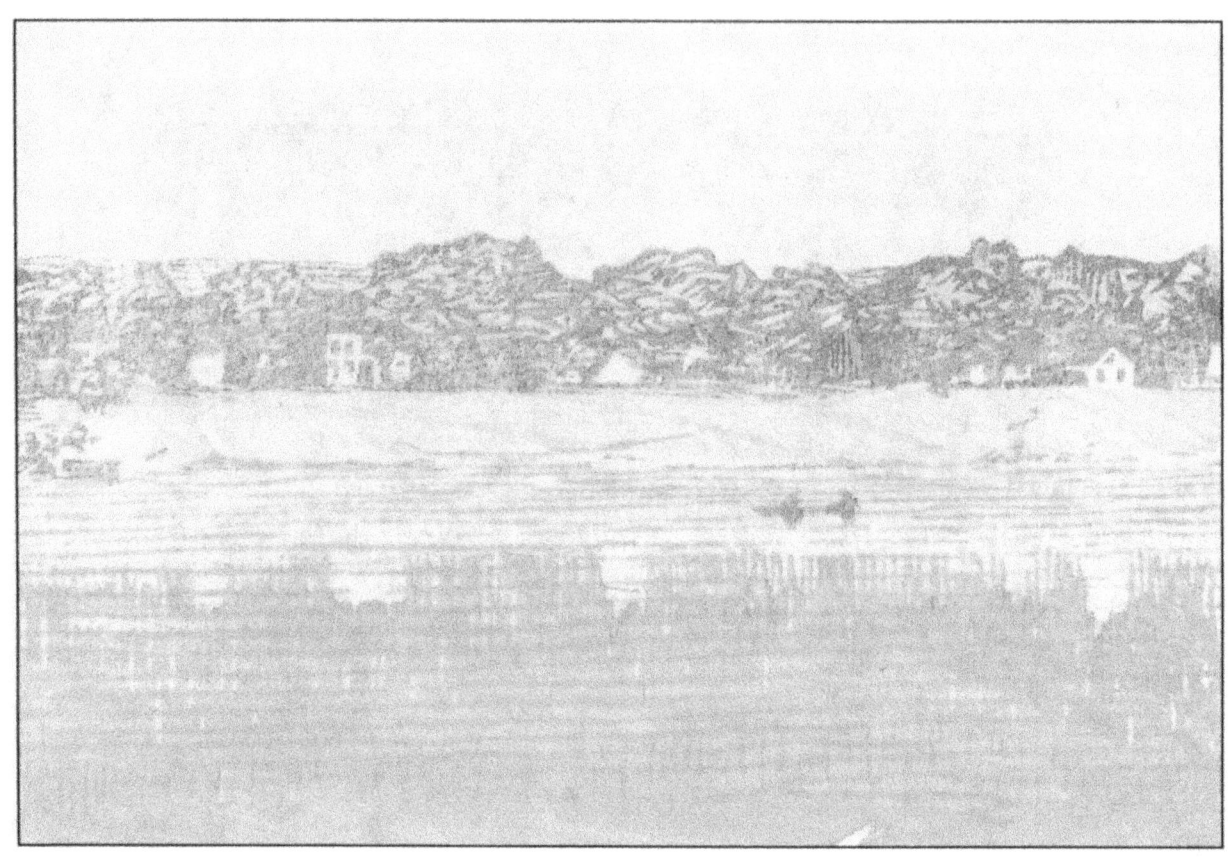

II Town and river

Sometimes when slowly paddling or drifting midway between the shores, I feel as detached in space as a mote in the atmosphere. The light from a sun infinitely far away strikes only me, it seems, my boat is cradled in water. I have no contact with the earth, which might well have vanished.

Journal, 1987

Hubbard also printed a black-only version of this.

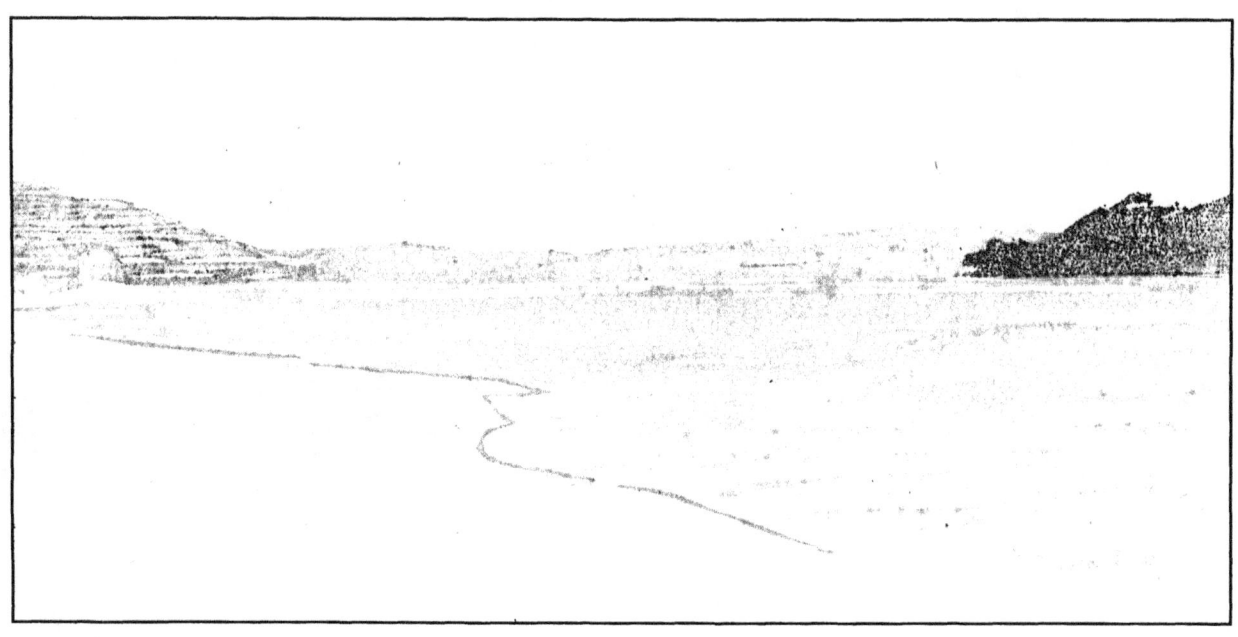

III   River shore

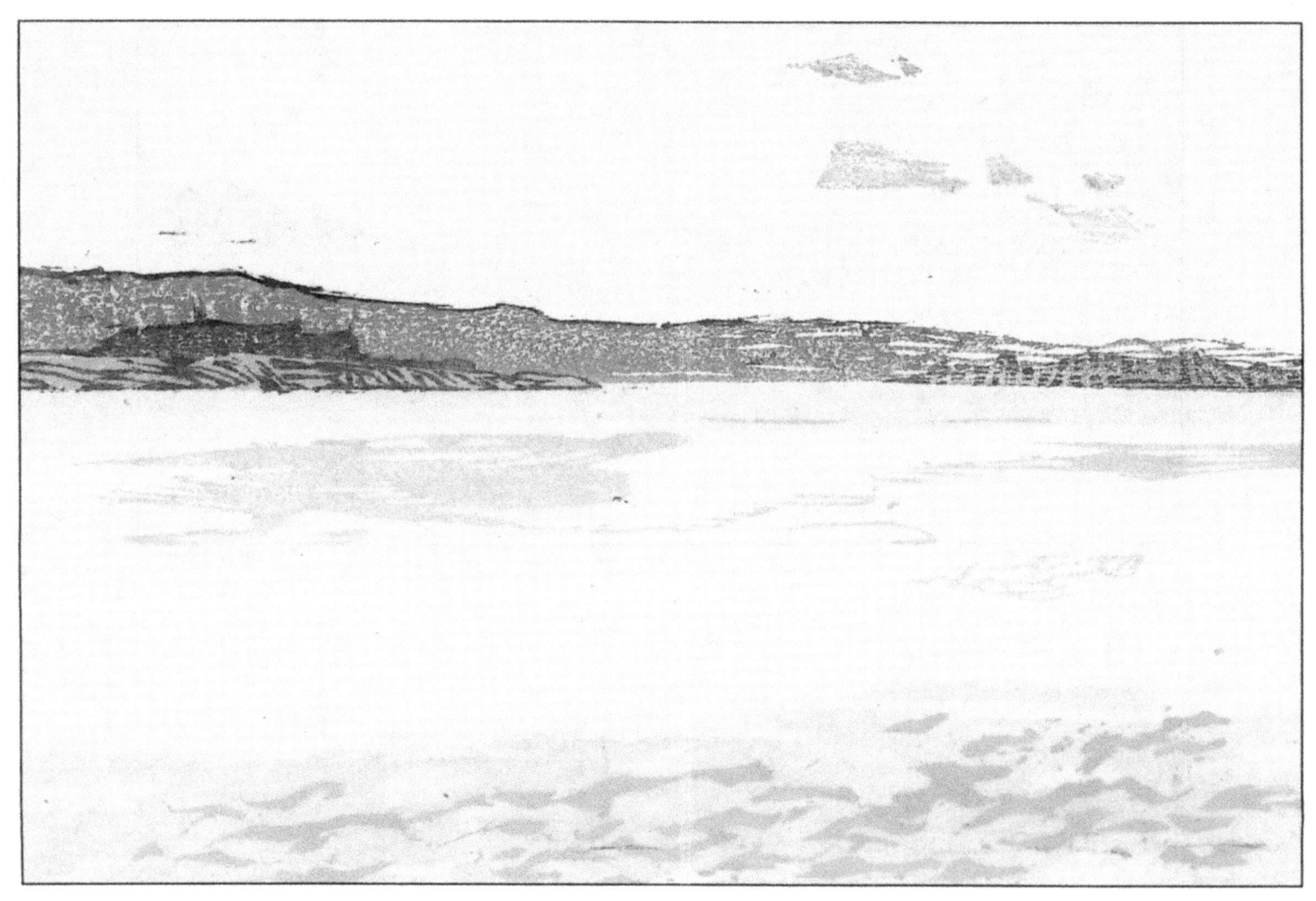

IV River scene

This harmony that I have known for so long—the sharp, chill air, the bare, blue hills, the rich, subdued colors of the budding trees, the swirling, muddy water, the sound of peepers, it is elemental, everlasting.

Journal, March 11, 1963

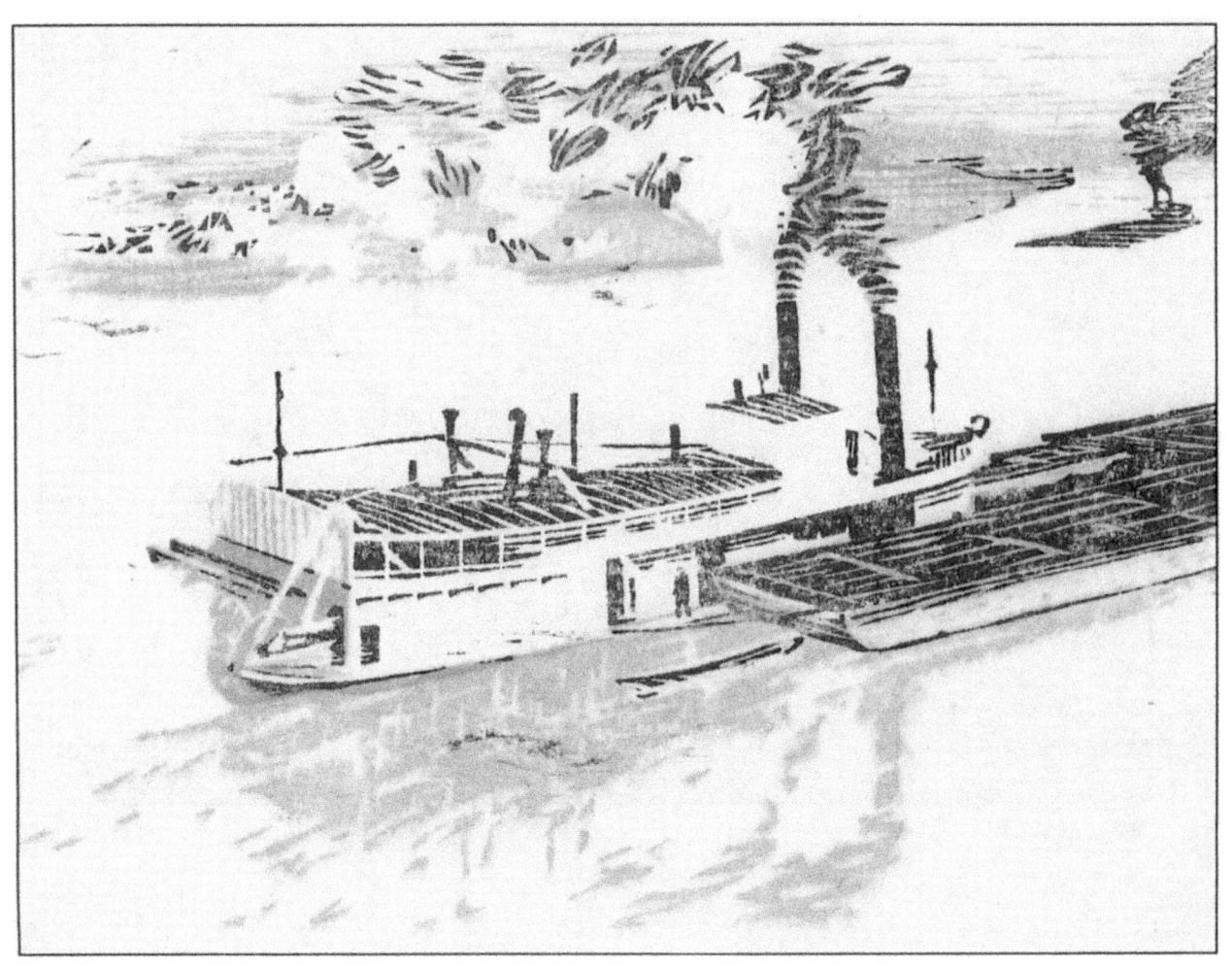

V Towboat with barges

One star on HH list. Hubbard's most elaborate print, seven colors, including white and cream. Faintly visible (dropping out of white on the boat's side) is "Harlan H."

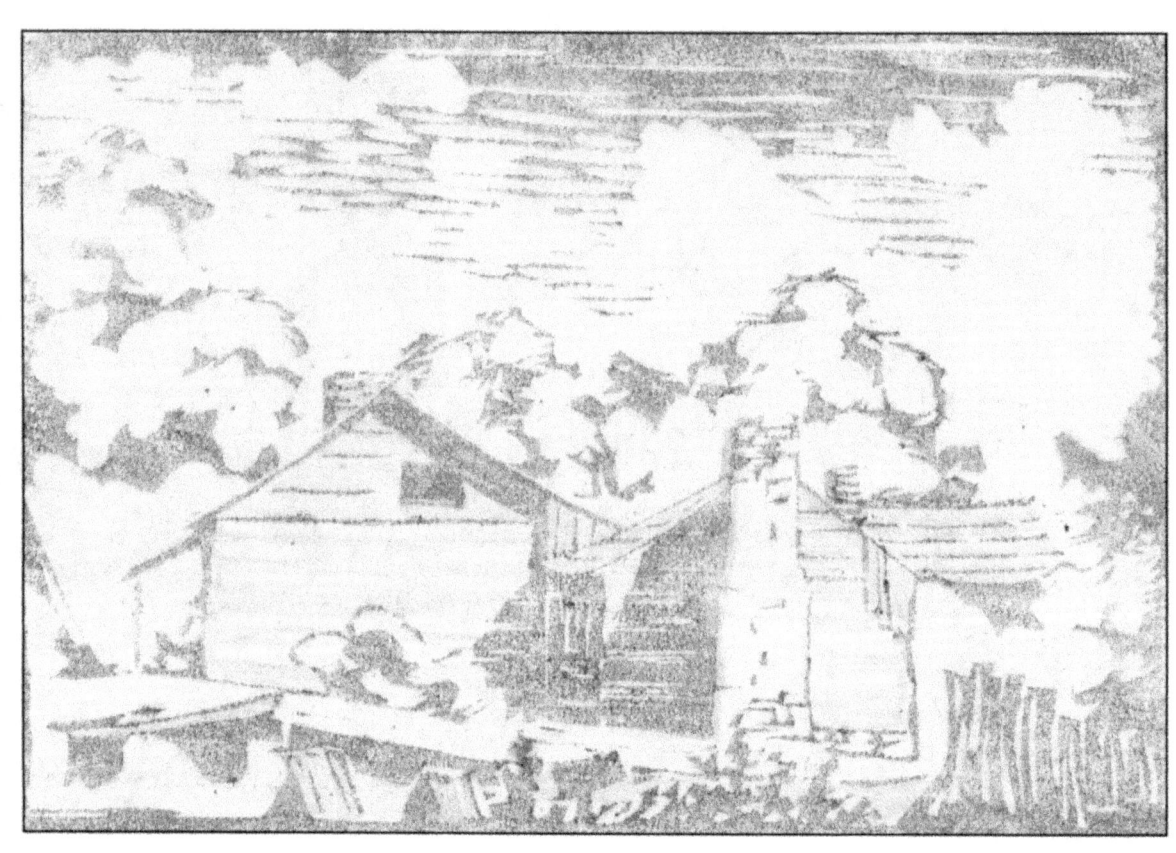

VI   Farmhouse in summer

One star on HH list.

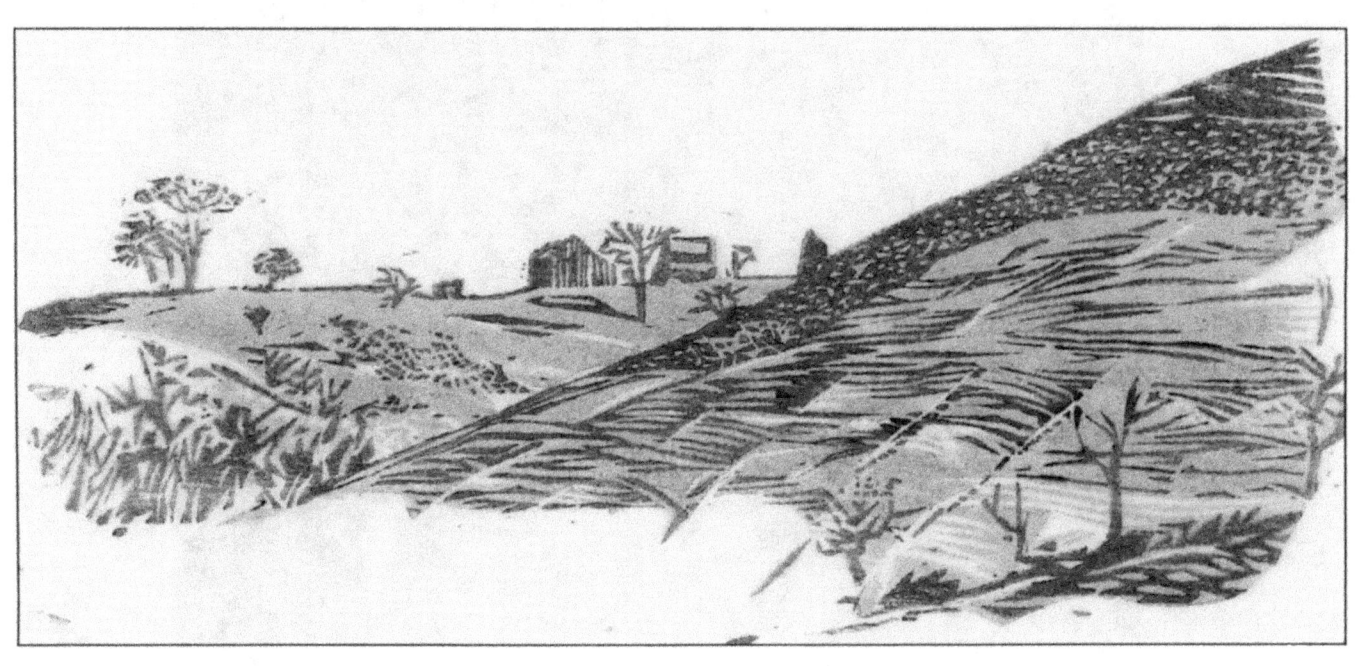

VII   Landscape with farm

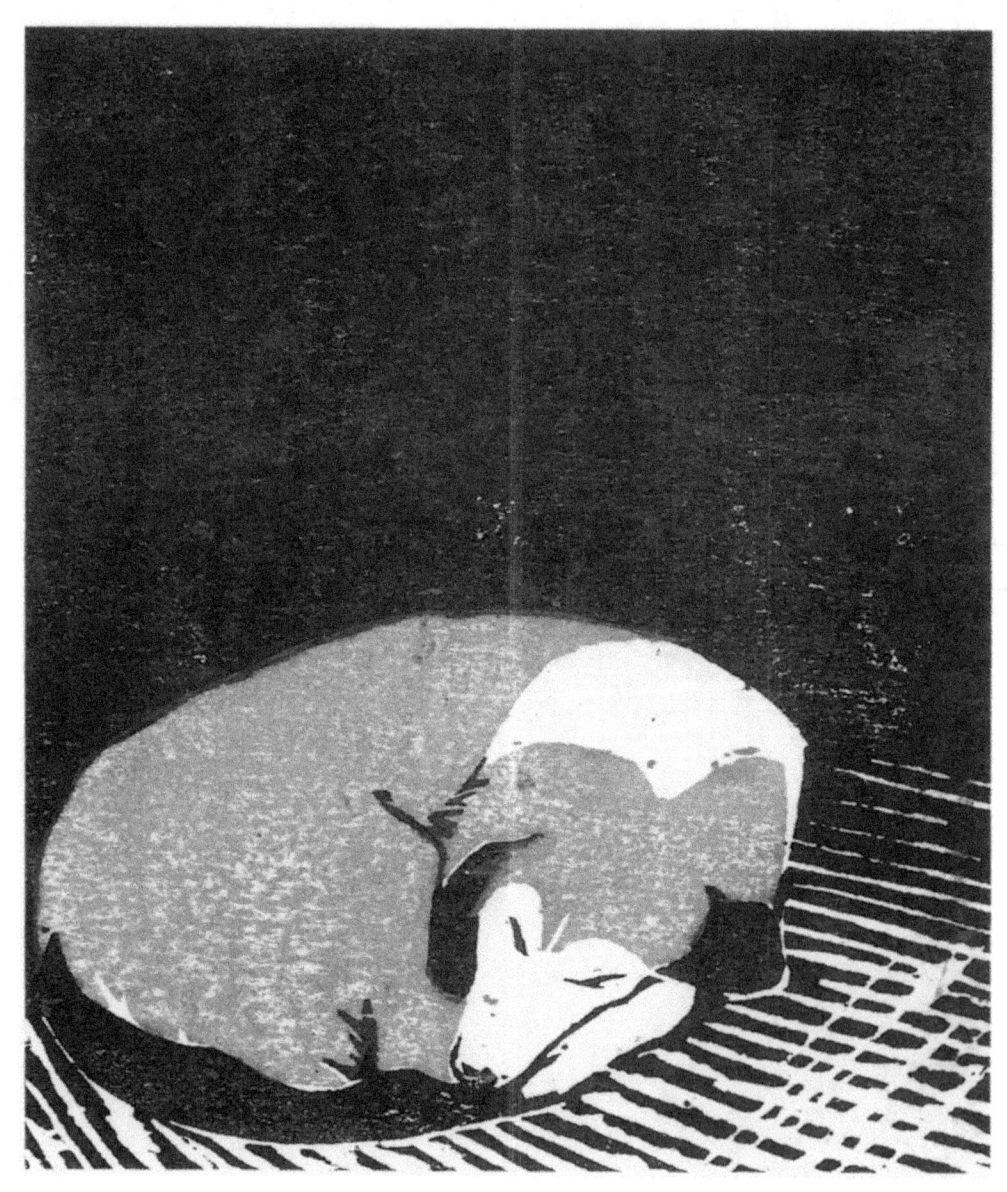

VIII Sleeping dog

On HH list.

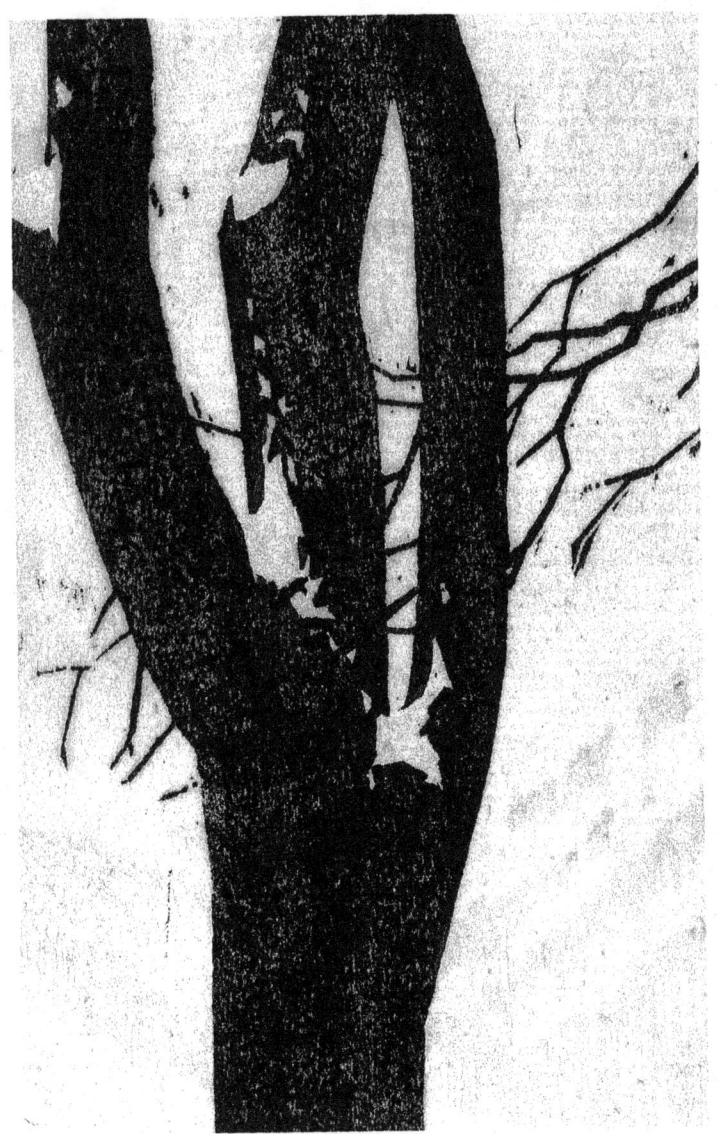

36 Tree trunk with snow

I enjoy over and over the repeated aspects of
nature. This is the foundation of my life.

Journal, July 2, 1963

One star on HH list. Printed with white ink as second color.

37 Brent, Kentucky

Life at Brent was to be such a rich experience in itself that it pleased us to remain there for a longer period than we had calculated. Perhaps all this was part of our adjustment to the tempo of the river, where time keeps pace with its slow current, where old things survive long past their day.

Shantyboat, pages 28-29

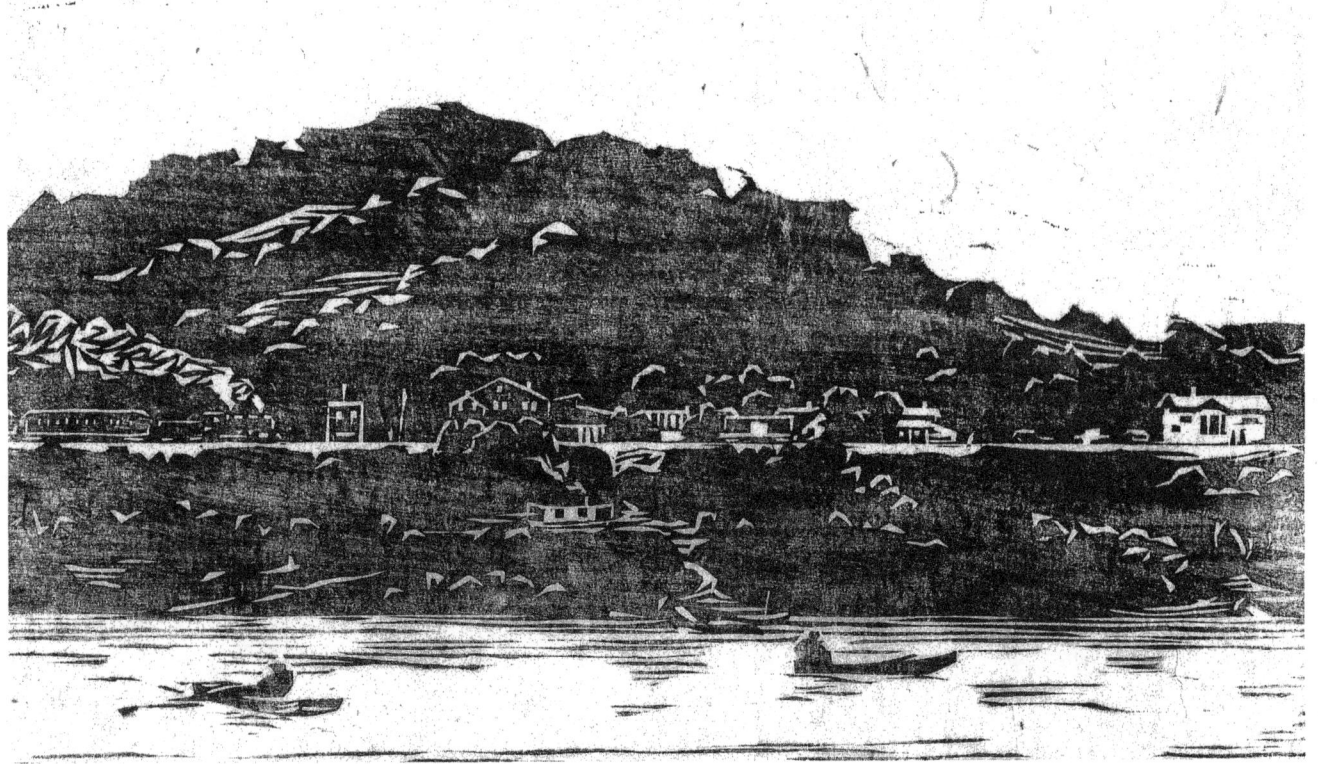

38   In the johnboat

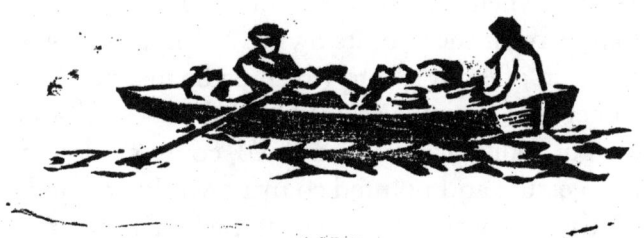

39   Conversing by lamplight

Sometimes of an evening we abandoned our fireside, made our way either by boat or along the shore path to our good neighbors, the Detisches. Their boat had the homey air of an old farmhouse kitchen, and a quaintness all its own. . . . Perhaps we would listen to a long yarn of Andy's, into which Sadie inserted her personal comments. There was an intensity about Andy's quiet, exact talk, but Sadie's was unrestrained, compounded of laughing and gesture and pointed country words, so good-humored that one would not suspect she had a care in the world.

Shantyboat, page 92

Original dimensions: 10¼" x 7¼".

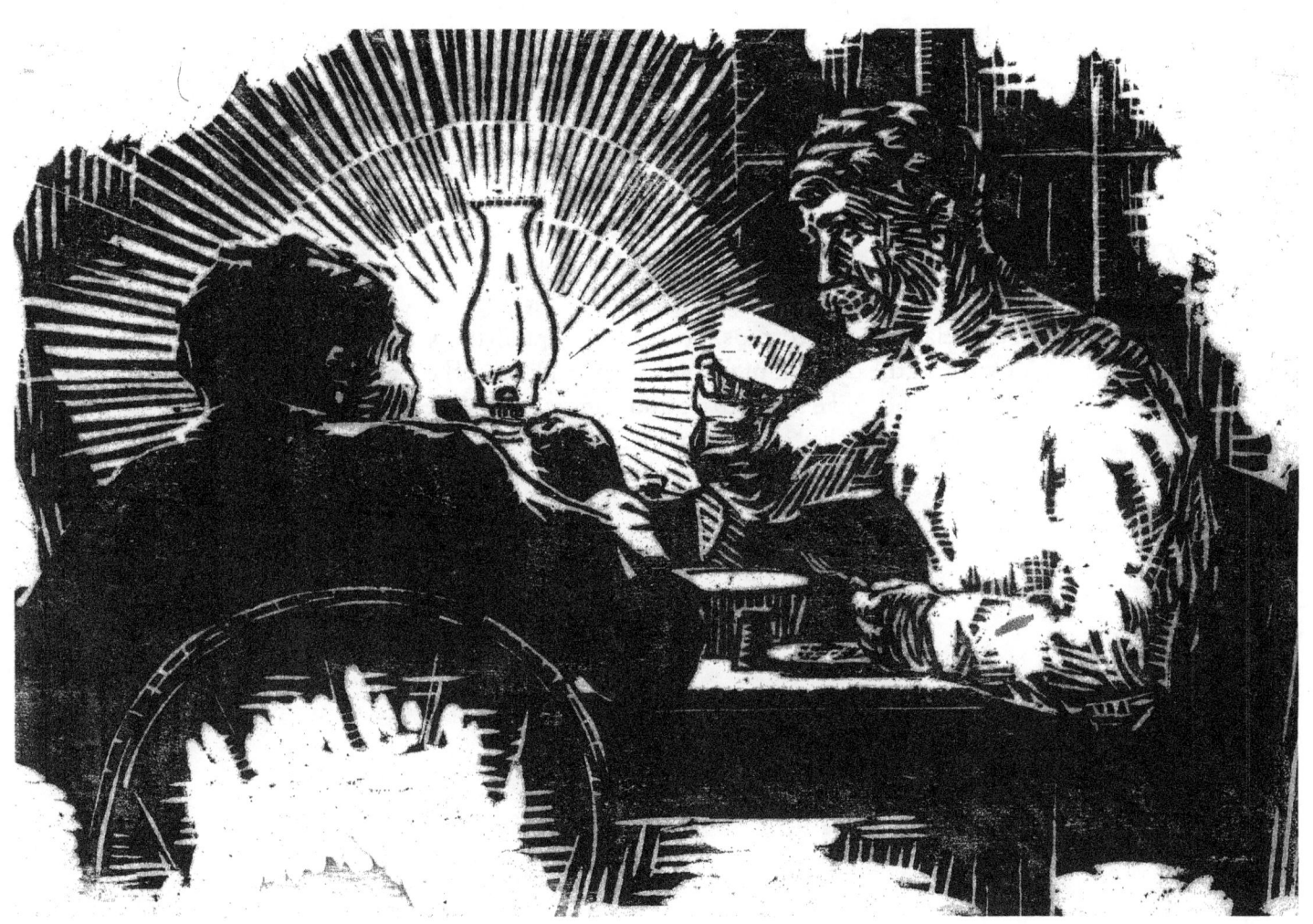

40 Ohio River

The sun rises and sets, it is day and night, it will go on thus for a long time. You get to think you are part of it and your circumstances are related to the cosmos, but one day your little system will break down and the day and night will rotate indifferently. Can this be? It seems more like the sunrise and sunset, the moon and stars, this new season, they are part of me. I am sure they will never be the same without me, for no one could see them just as I do.

Journal, March 9, 1963

Christmas card, 1946. Hand signed in pencil.

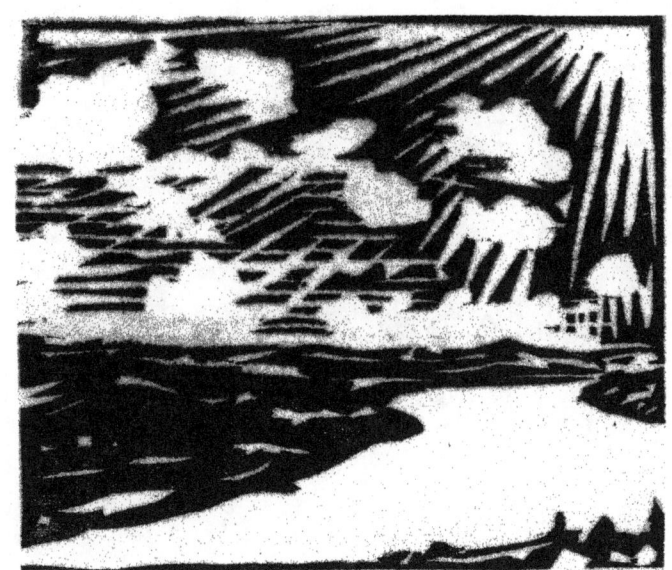

Anna and Harlan Hubbard

41 River town

On HH list.

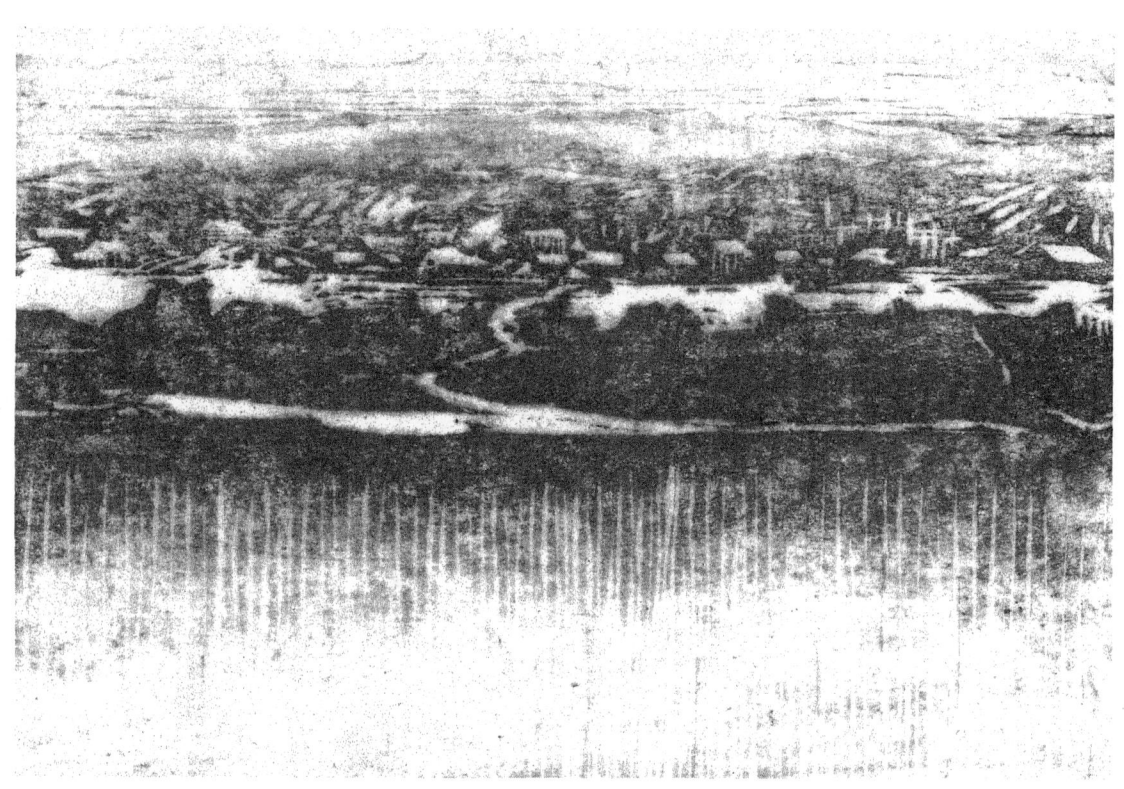

42   The Hubbard shantyboat trapped in ice

The winter weather was glorious. The river of ice sparkled
under the bright sun and moon. . . . Then came a day when
the slow pace of the floating river became a new creation,
a vast snowy plain, its smooth surface broken by low
heaps and ridges of ice. . . . a Siberian landscape.

Shantyboat, page 167

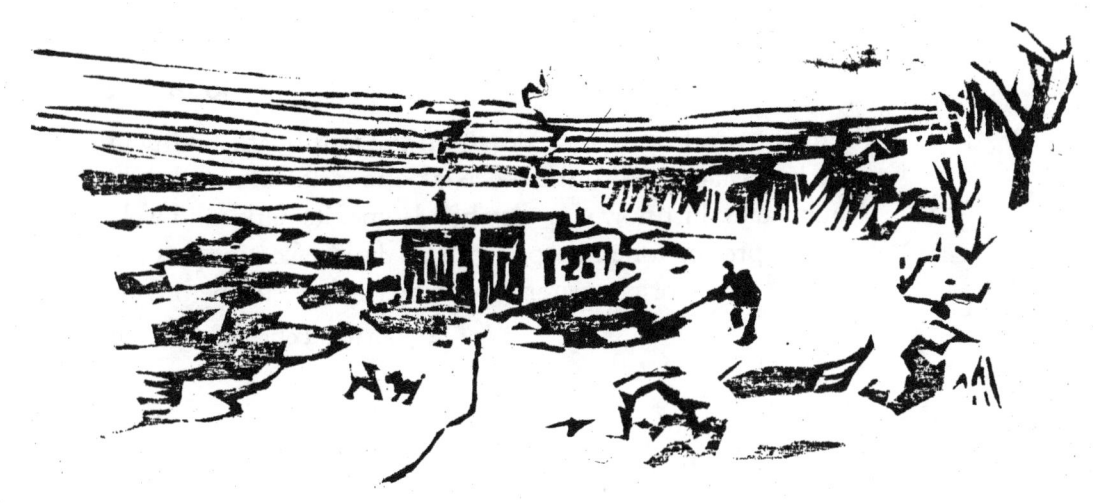

43 Johnboat

From our window we look down on the johnboat floating in
the backwater, tied to the fence, a patient, loved member of
our estate. Just now it is very handsome, its dark solid well-
proportioned shape, with its dark reflection, on the
bright water lighted by the low sun before us.

Journal, February 19, 1959

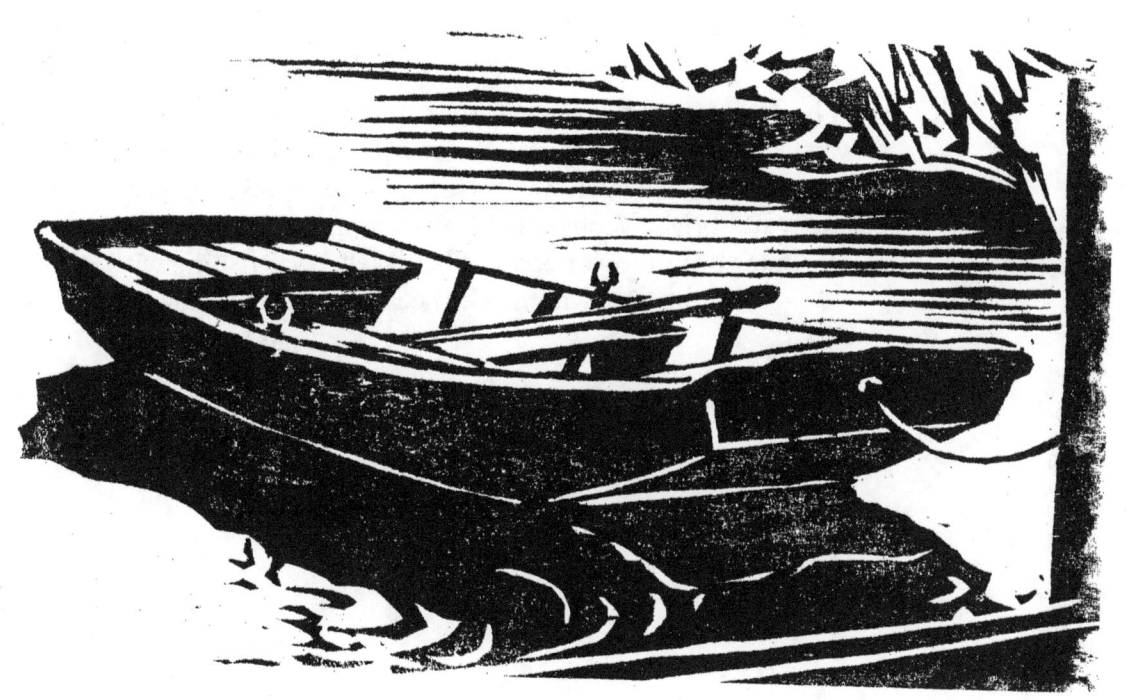

44 Running a trotline

When finished, I put out the light, and rowing slowly back,
watched Cassiopeia rising in the eastern sky. She seemed to
draw up her fish line, which was Perseus, with the misty Pleiades
as bait, and bright Venus caught. All was growing dim in the
faint beginning of dawn. Then I felt I was fishing with
the One who made the river and set it flowing.

Shantyboat, page 74

Printed in black and gray.

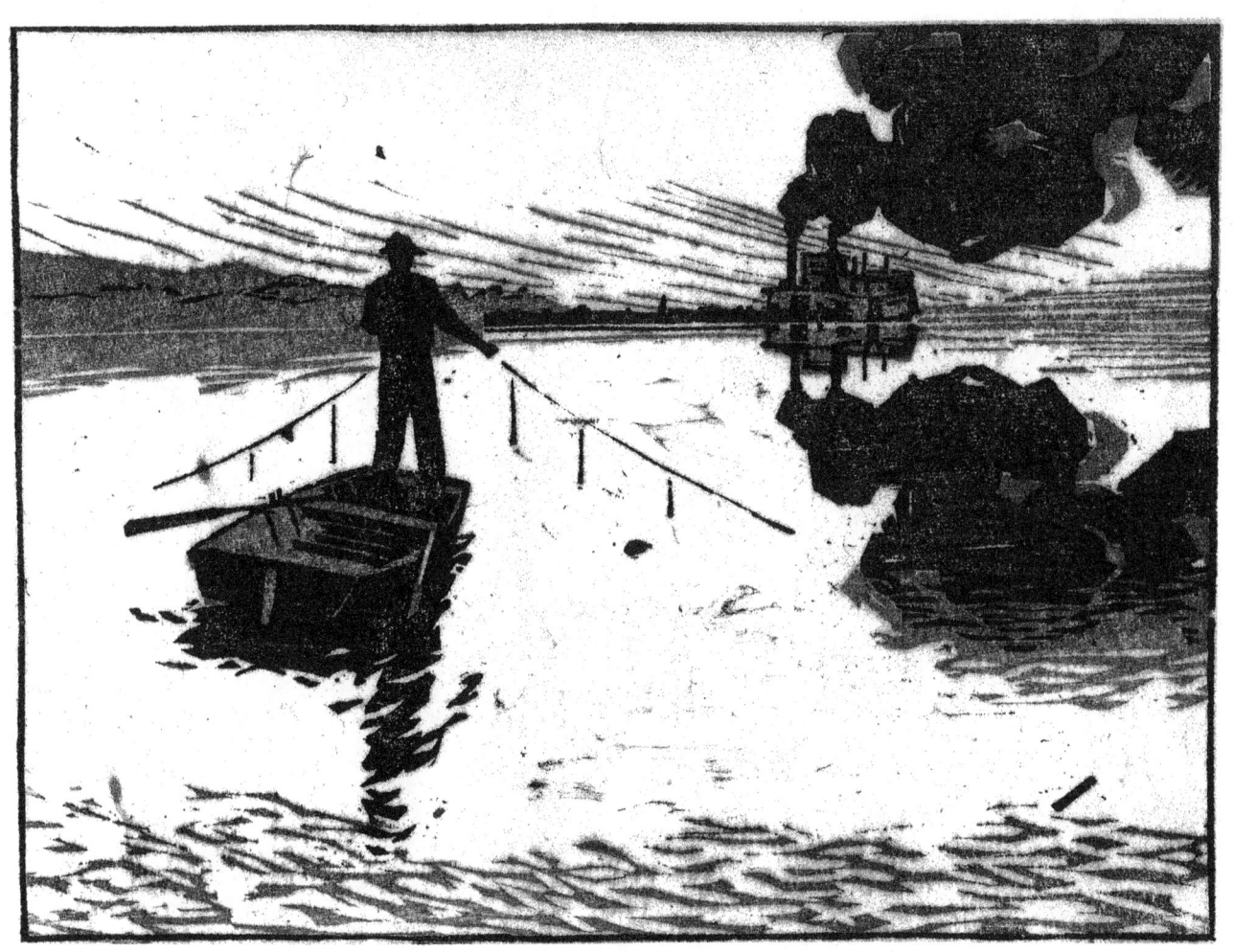

45 Hill farm by night

I made gleanings, too, which were far different from those
I had set out to find. My eyes roamed the earth's uneven
surface, feeling each slant and texture, or into the sky among
its titanic sculptures. Nowhere was chaos, but all was bound
up in a harmony which was so strongly felt at times that
the scene before me seemed no longer earthly.

Shantyboat, page 78

Printed in black and gray.

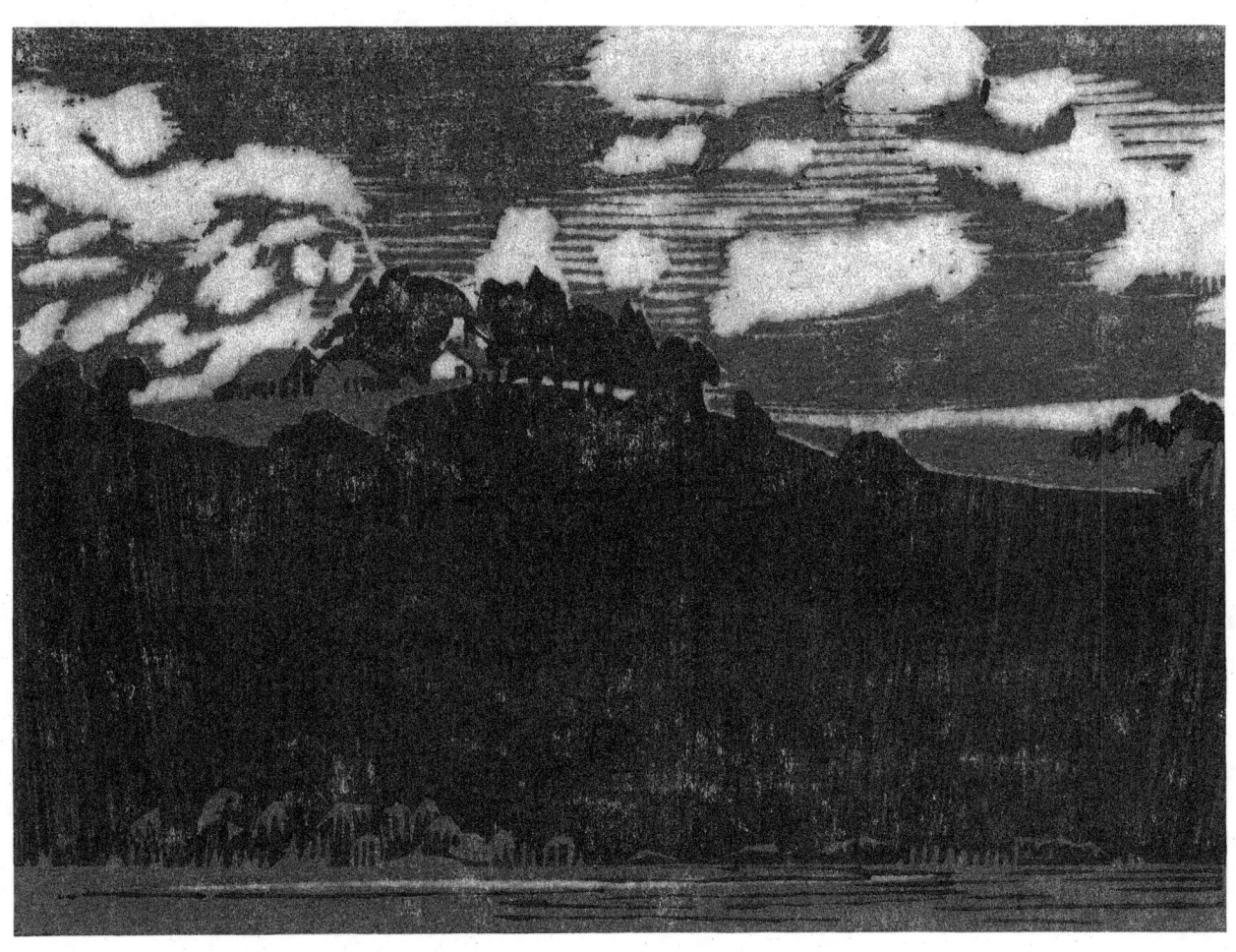

46 On the shantyboat, summer

Drifting became a passion with us in the four winters of our trip
down the Ohio and Mississippi rivers. During the quiet intervals
of summer we were content to lay over at some rural landing with
at least one foot on shore, where we made a garden and became
for the time members of the farm community around us.

Shantyboat on the Bayous, page 2

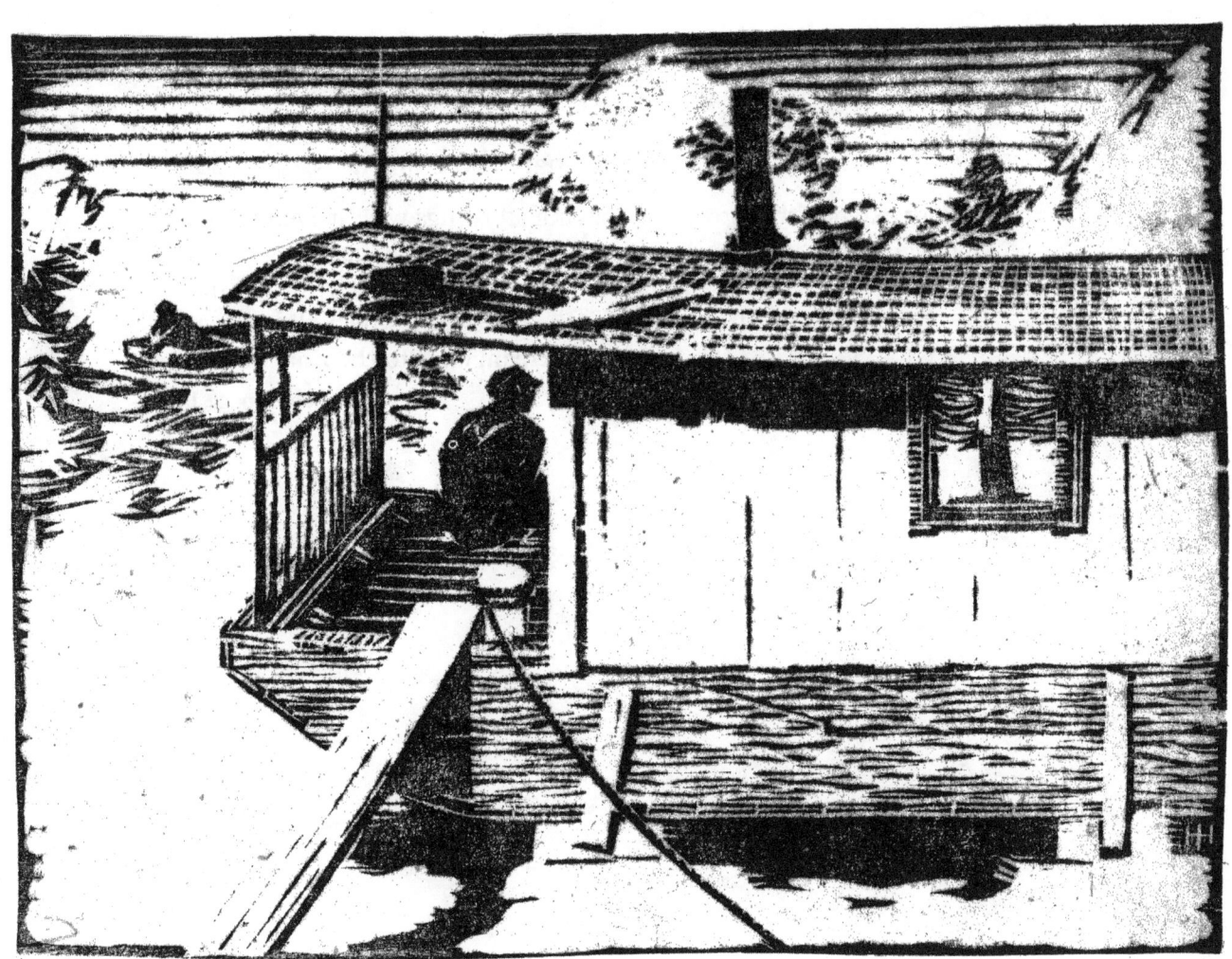

47   The Hubbard shantyboat on the Mississippi

The river extends this power of drawing all things with it even to the
imagination of those who live on its banks. Who can long watch
the ceaseless lapsing of a river's current without conceiving a desire
to set himself adrift, and, like the driftwood which glides past,
float with the stream clear to the final ocean?

Shantyboat, page 1

Christmas card, 1949.

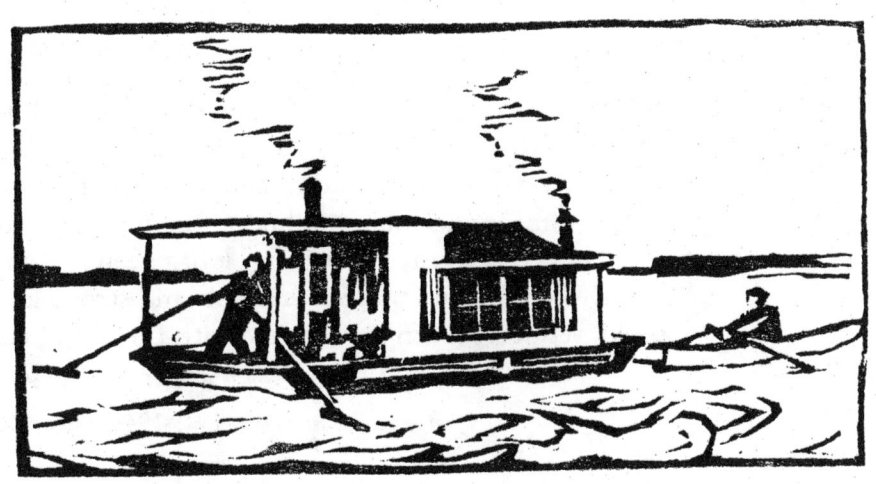

48 Mississippi River levee

I was not satisfied unless the picture was real—in the thin air, with true surfaces construction and proportion. At the same time I could see an inward design, two-dimensional and abstract, in mass and color and line, springing up, even though I did not consciously put it there. It has been my aim to foster this design and make it as simple and strong as I could, yet never letting it interfere with the objective.

December 5, 1935

Journals, 1929-1944, page 120

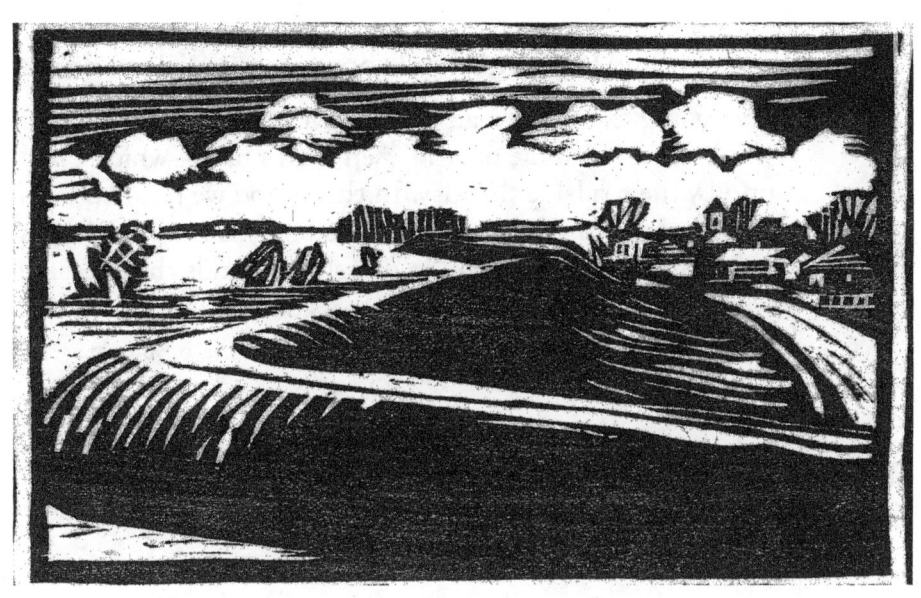

49 The Hubbard shantyboat on a Louisiana bayou

Before going to bed we read a little in a tattered fragment of a book—once a volume of Andersen's fairy tales—which I had found by the roadside that day. In this mood we recalled tales and legends of the bayous, heard along the river or read in forgotten books, and in our sleepy minds they became enchanted streams leading into a country beyond reality.

Shantyboat on the Bayous, page 10

Christmas card, 1950.

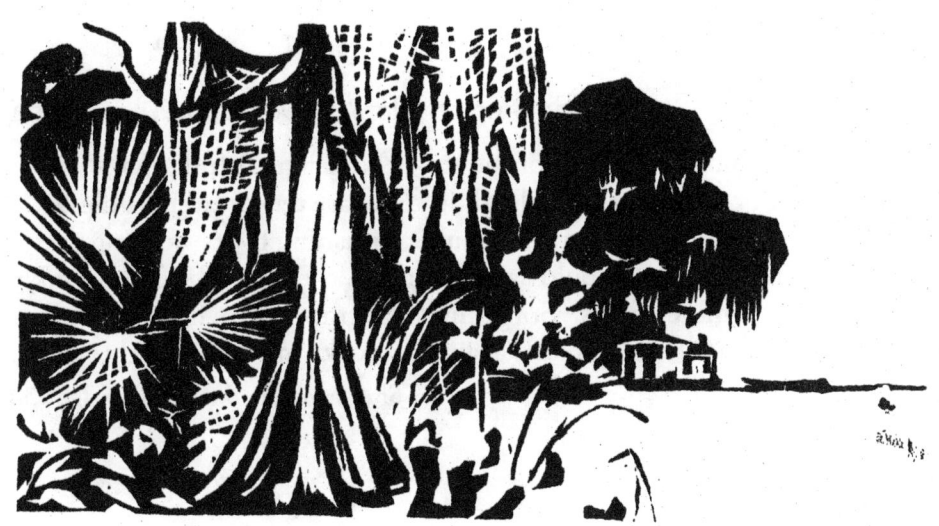

50   Shrimp trawlers in Delcambre, Louisiana

Delcambre is another of the small Louisiana fishing ports which
are not on the coast but inland, in this case ten or twelve miles. . . .
If I were to guess at the number of fishing boats working out of
Delcambre, I would say a hundred; there may be considerably
more or less. Sometimes the trawlers are lined up two or
three abreast, again the docks might be nearly vacant.

Shantyboat on the Bayous, page 130

Two stars on HH list. Hubbard considered this one of his three best prints,
the others being 51 and 73. Original dimensions: 8 ¼" x 3".

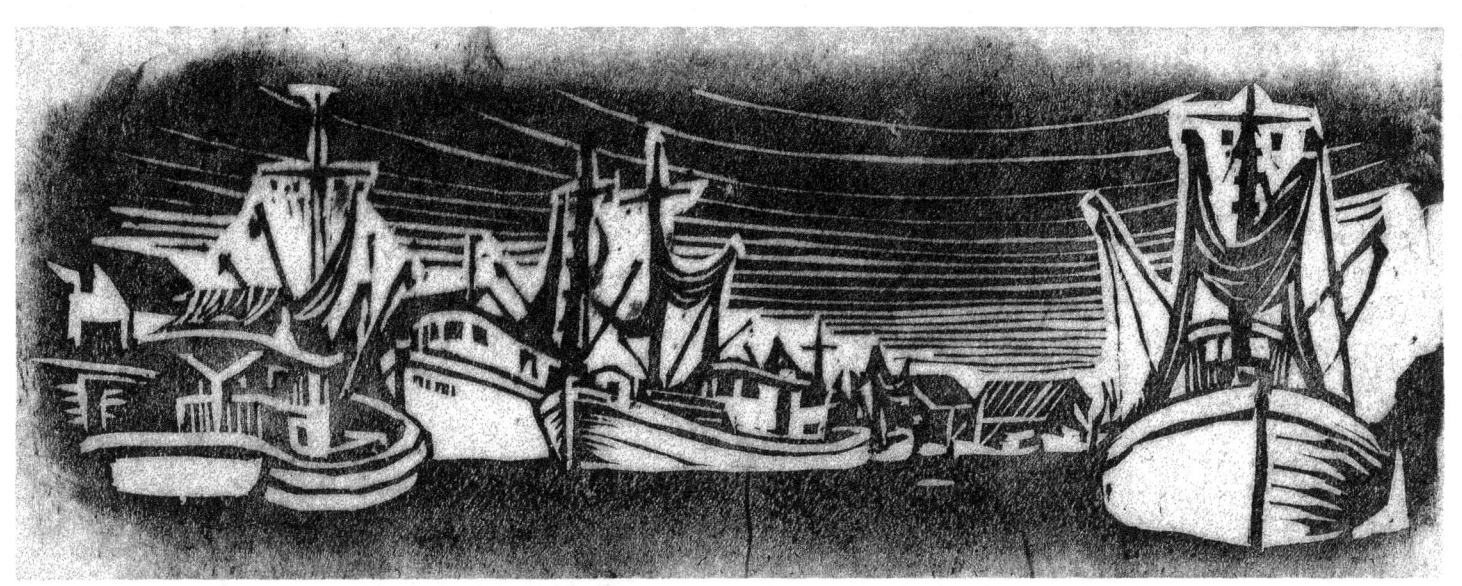

51 St. Martinsville Church, Louisiana

Two stars on HH list. Hubbard considered this his best print.

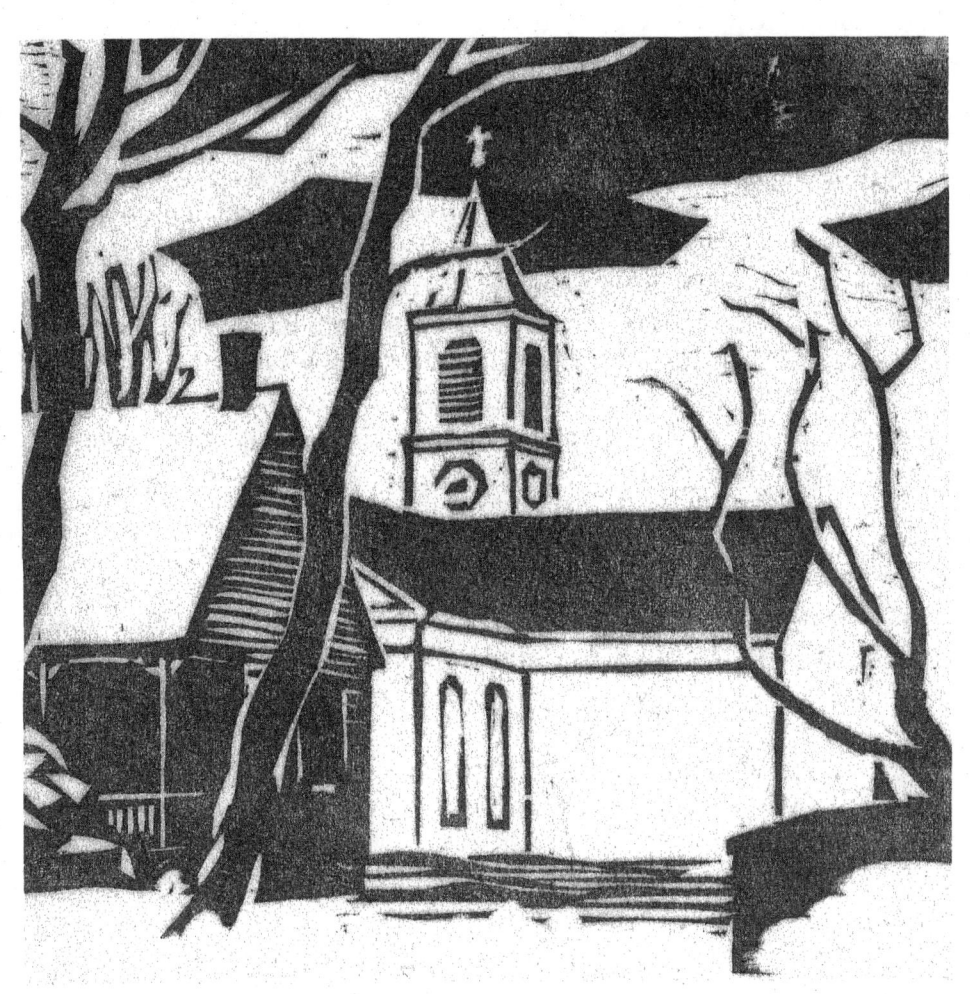

52   Boatload of neighbors and shrimpboat, Louisiana bayous

A boatload of eight or ten varied youngsters passed us every morning
on their way to meet a school bus on the highway, returning in the
afternoon. Evidently the mothers pooled their children, for each
day a different lady was rowing expertly at the stand-up oars of the
pushing skiff. Sometimes on the return trip one of the children—
having begged for the honor, no doubt—was at the heavy oars,
though they could hardly be reached by short arms.

Shantyboat on the Bayous, page 94

Printed by Konrad Juestel.

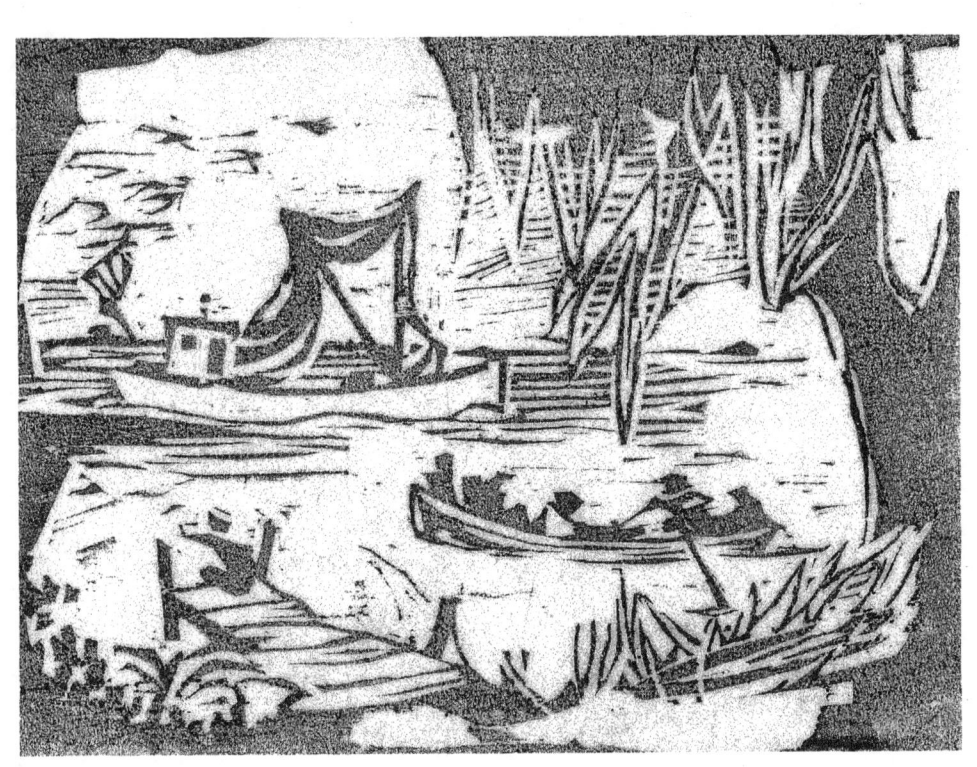

53 Mountains, California

Harlan and Anna reached California early in 1952.
Two stars on HH list.

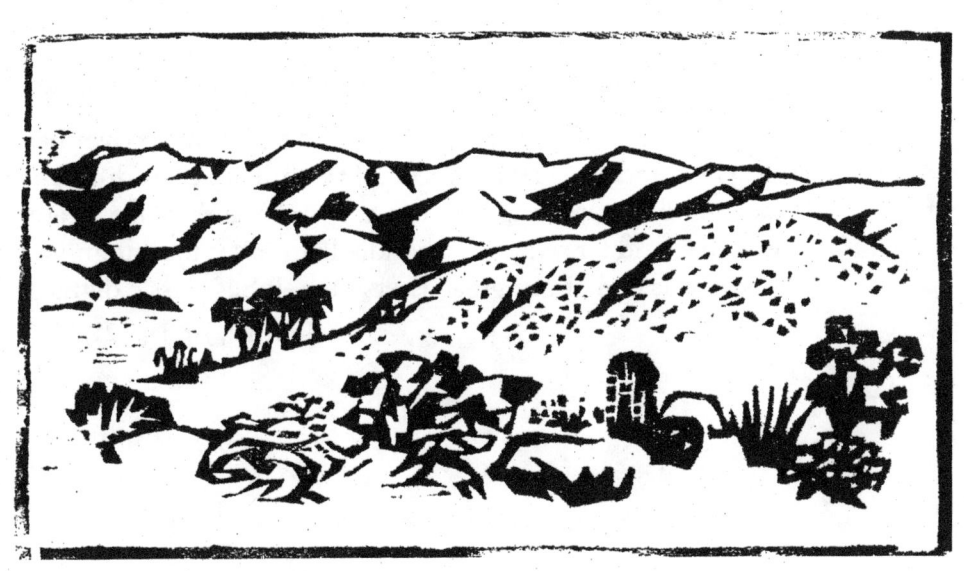

54 View up the Ohio from Payne Hollow, with Plowhandle Point at left

I go down to bail out the johnboat, and the view up river has something of grandeur. The mist sets off the hills to their different distances, and the opening between the two points is like a gateway to a land far away. Plowhandle Point rises mountainlike. This view is one of our great assets here. It has classic dignity.

Journal, January 21, 1962

Two stars on HH list. Printed in medium gray blue.

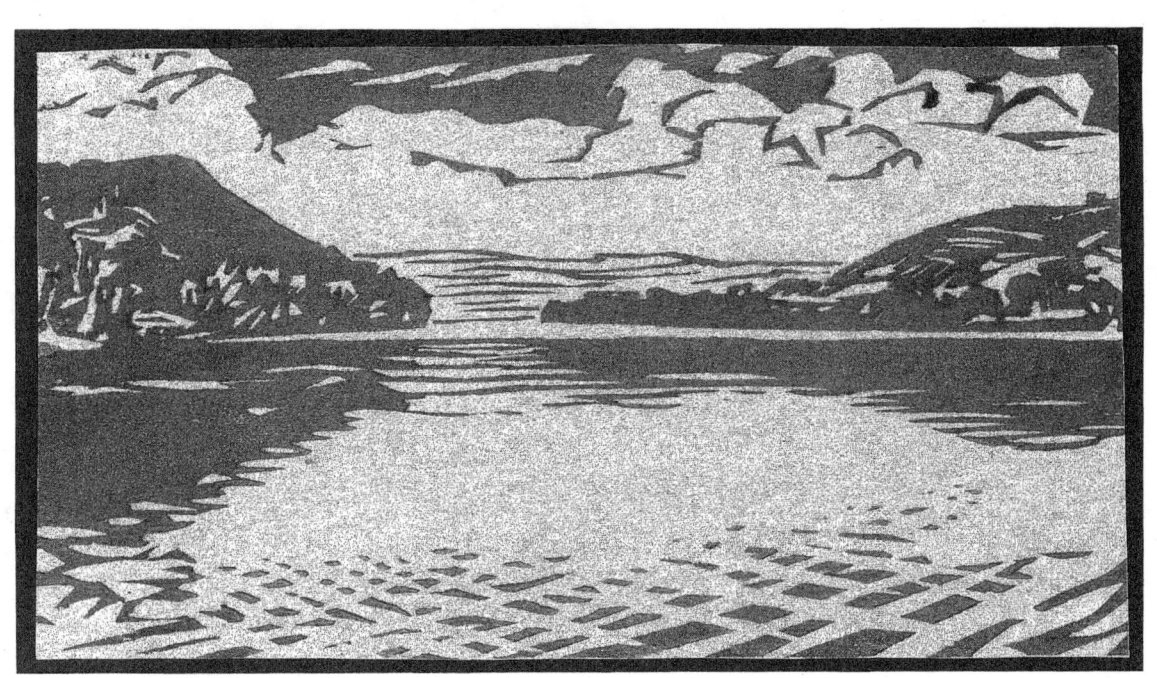

55 Harlan's workshop at Payne Hollow before he built the studio

Perhaps the time will come when I will not be here in Payne Hollow,
will not even be active and out of doors so I will write about these
days, about what now seems trivial doings, about the weather, the way
the river looks under different skies, writing to myself changed and at a
later time, trying to put a little of these days into words which may
sometime mean more than they do now, and give an essence of the
life that passed here—more concentrated and definite perhaps
in a distance of time and space than I now feel.

Journal, November 1, 1959

Original dimensions: 7 ⅜" x 9 ¾".

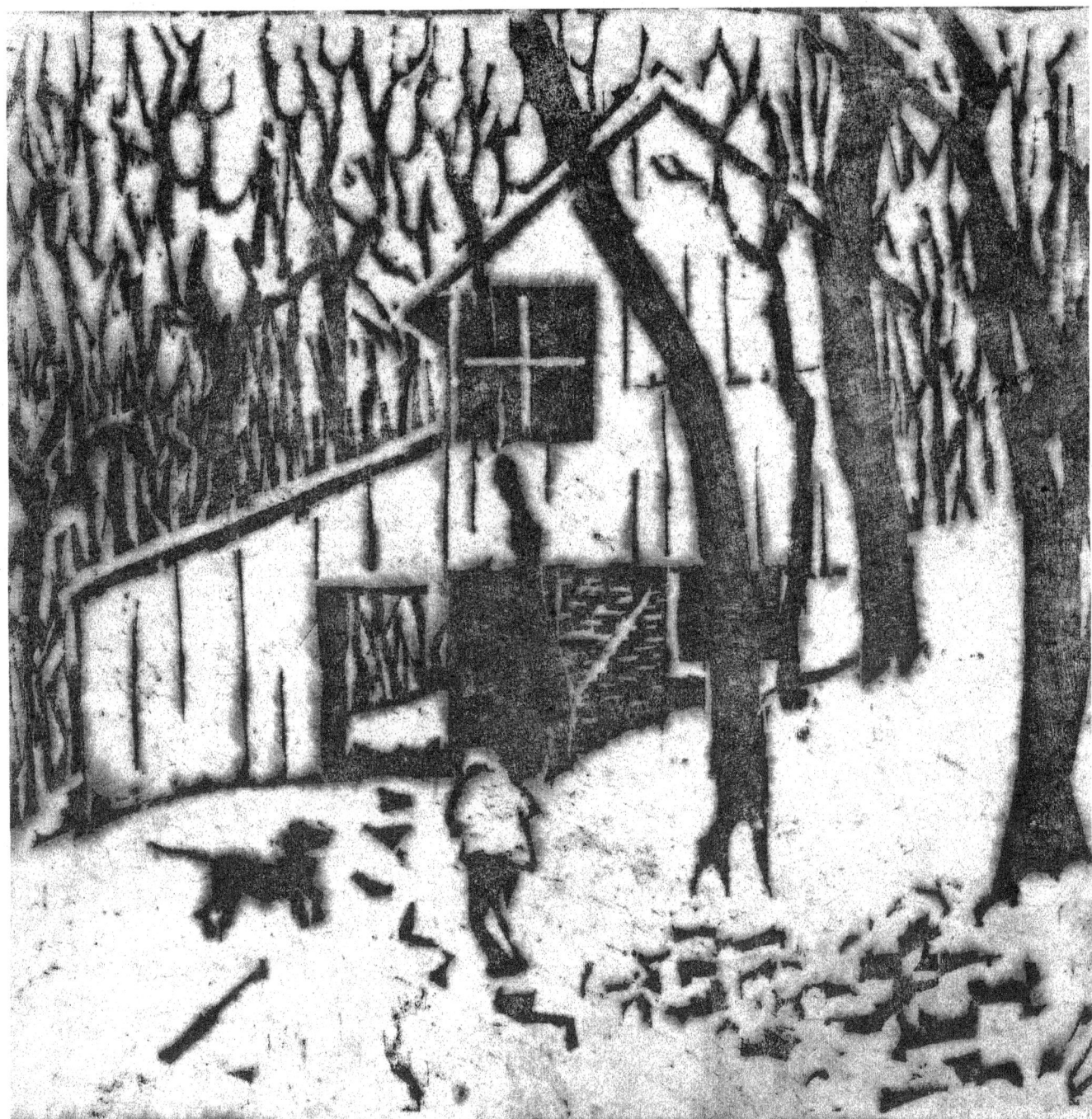

56   Lee's Landing in the snow

The river was calm and smooth, the three stars of Orion's belt
reflected in the water just over the johnboat. The simple
masses of night's landscape. I went out along the path
and began to saw firewood as the light of the coming
day began to show in the east.

It was 20° this morning, well below 40 all day.

Journal, December 8, 1961

Christmas card, 1953

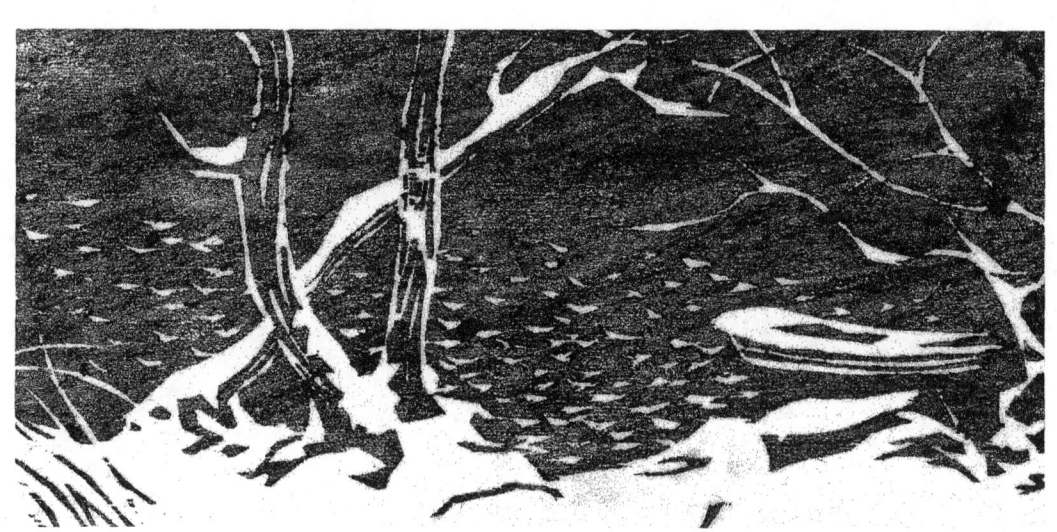

57   Steamboat

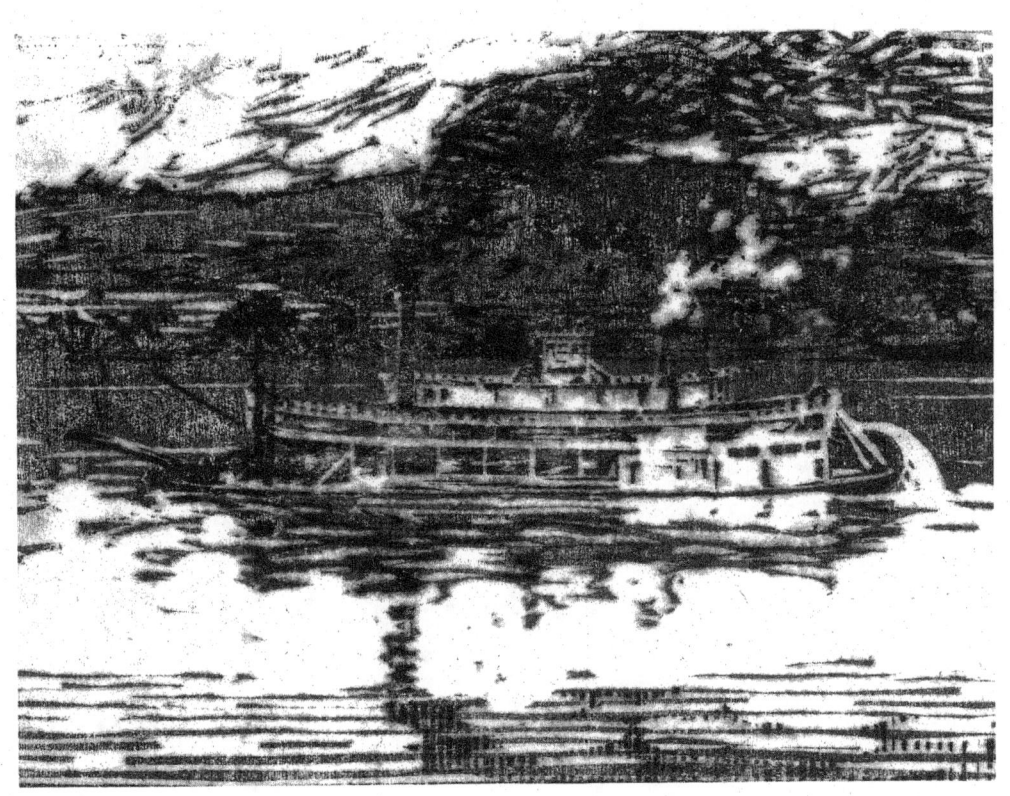

58   Trees in snow

Probably no moon has furnished me with as much light as this one, in this clear weather. Now it is past full, and I can arise before daybreak and see my way about, sawing firewood. One feels alone on the earth, no sounds, no lights, anywhere, unless a boat passes. In a light fog, as this morning, the isolation is even more strongly felt. It brings peace, contentment and a sure faith that all is well.

Journal, December 28, 1958

Christmas card, date unknown. Two stars on HH list.

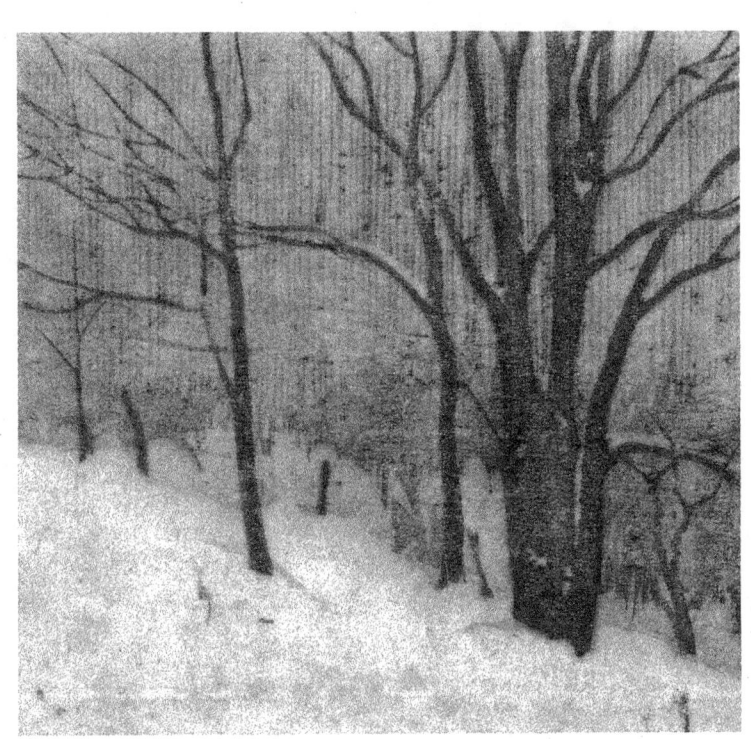

59   Payne Hollow mailbox

To us Payne Hollow is the center of the world,
to all others, it is on the farthest border.

Journal, September 3, 1959

Christmas card, 1955.

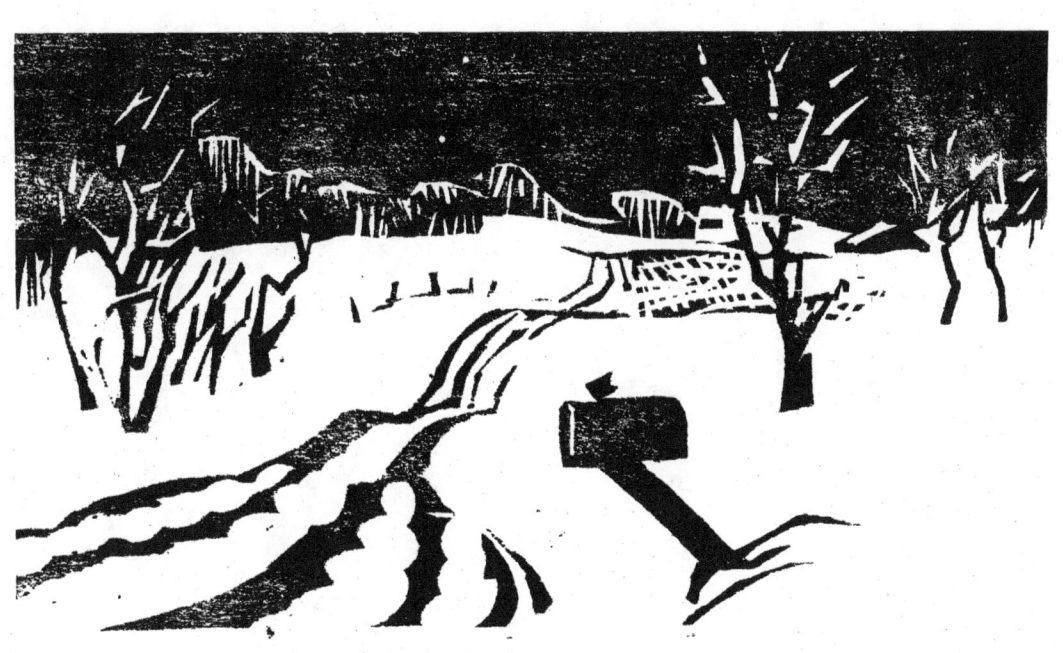

60 River by moonlight

What church or shrine could be as holy and comforting
as the river was this dark evening?

Journal, December 12, 1963

Two stars on HH list.

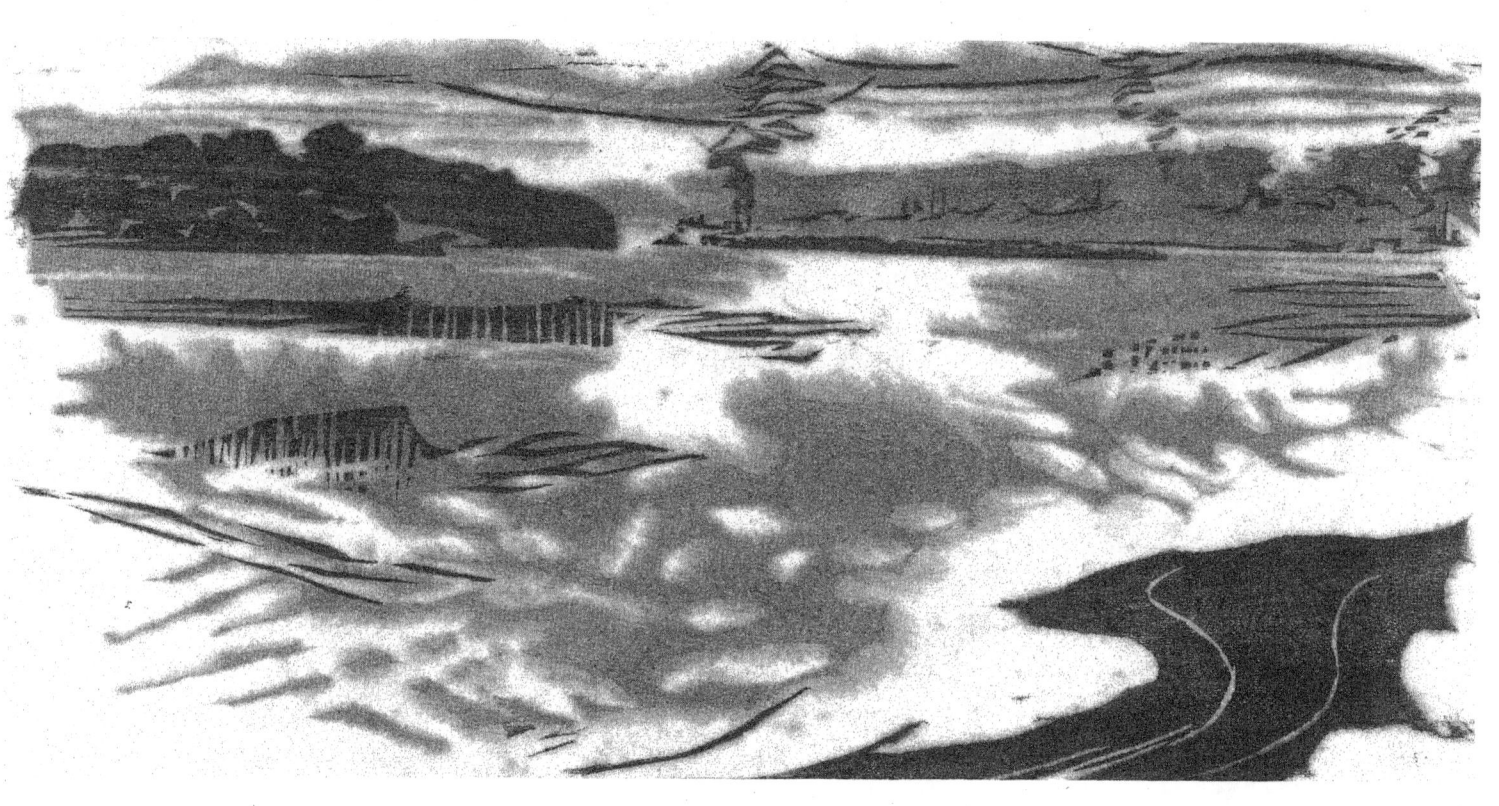

61 Summer landscape

Part of the beauty of the landscape is due to cultivated fields
and bare spaces. You wouldn't want everything to be trees
exactly, or rock. Any landscape, no man is worthy of it. It has
a beauty man's life never has. It's something to aspire to.
That's one thing I try to express in my painting.

Burdine, *Harlan Hubbard,* page 5

On HH list.

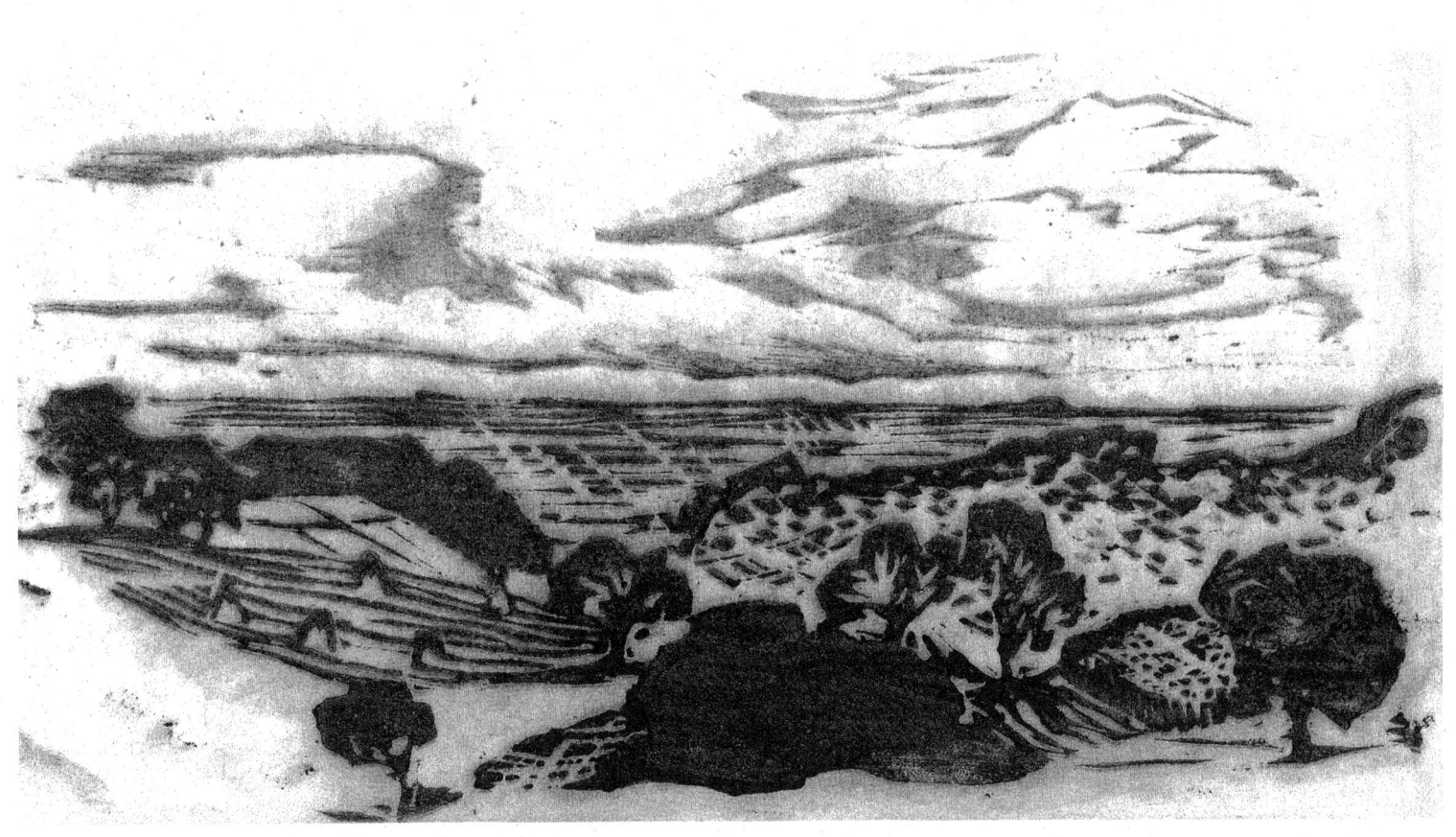

62   The house at Payne Hollow, winter

We are thankful for shelter and warmth and abundant food,
warm clothing: yet all this alone would not give us much
satisfaction or happiness. This comes from wood fires,
from food almost as natural as wood burning, from the
satisfaction of having cut your own wood, produced
your own food, built a house just for ourselves.

Journal, December 1, 1966

Hand dated "59?" by Hubbard (but see Print 72). Presumed to be a
Christmas card because of the wreath on the door.

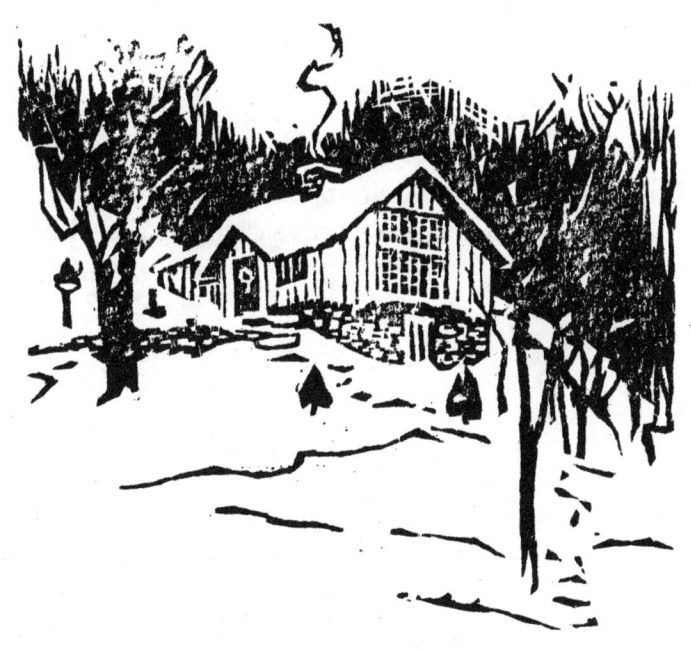

63 Man's head

Is not one man by himself important and worth consideration?
To me he is worth sacrificing the whole world for.

Journal, May 17, 1963

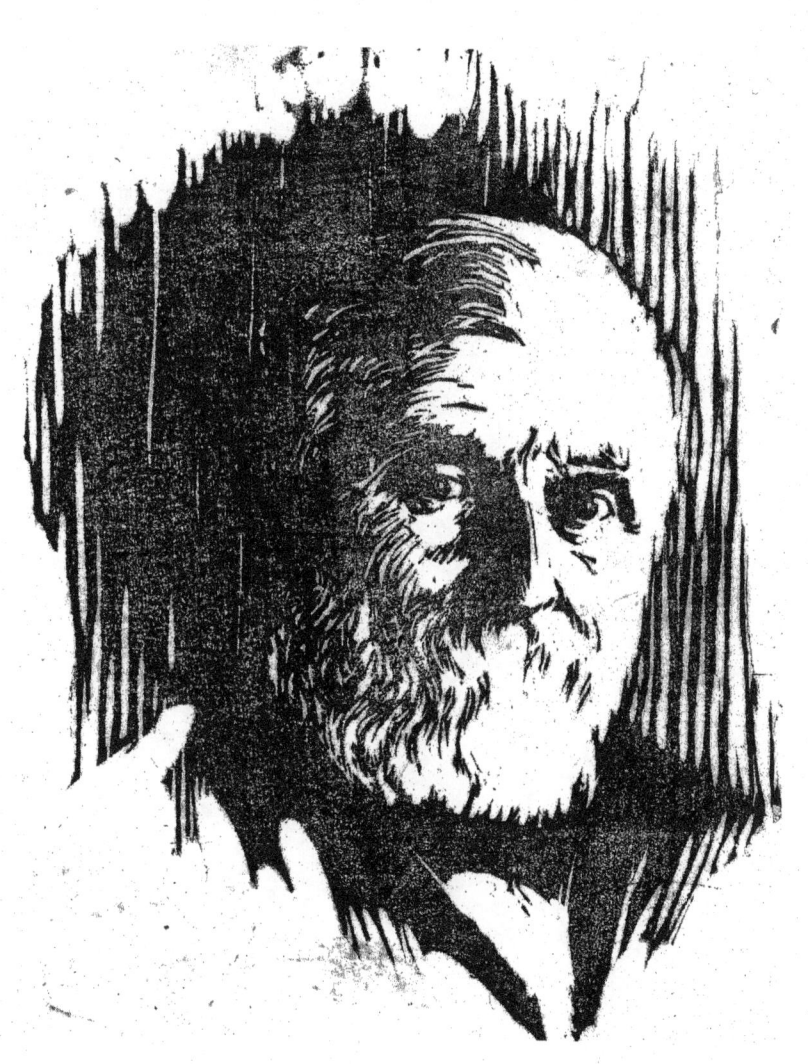

64   Towboat with barges

One attribute of the steamboat, both packet and towboat, I sorely
miss: their whistles. Some of these sounded beautiful chords that
echoed from the hills, filling the valley with wild music.

Journals, 1929-1944, page 51

On HH list.

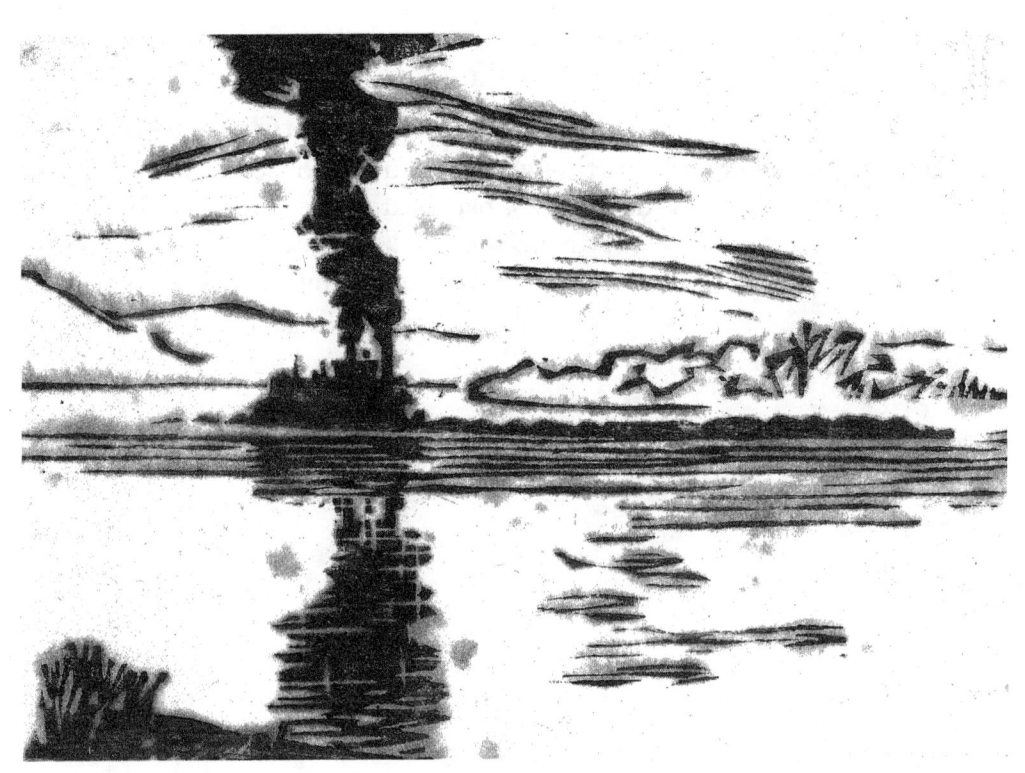

65 Plowhandle Point from Payne Hollow

Man's life on this earth—who has courage to face it? Yet there are
the trees, against the dark sky, black bare trees, springing from the
earth to flower, swaying in the wind, the low moan of the wind.
Who could live without this grace?

Journal, December 17, 1964

Christmas card, 1962. Hand signed in pencil.

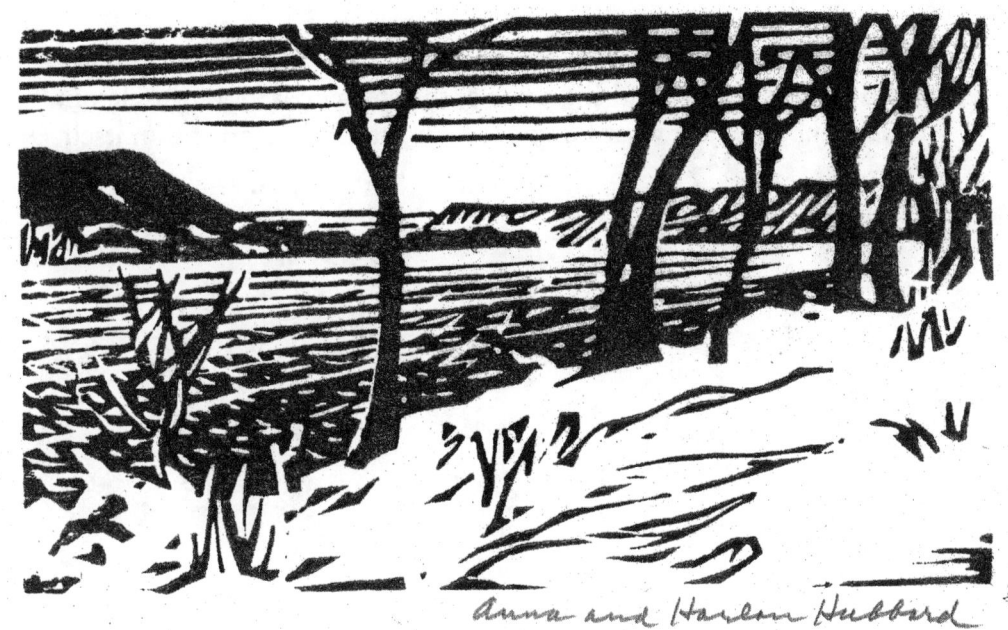

Anna and Harlan Hubbard

66   Towboat *Wacuta*

I try to express the life and character of the steamboat, not its skeleton.
It is a symbol, of just what I do not know, rather than an end in itself.

Journal, June 7, 1965

Printed in black and gray.

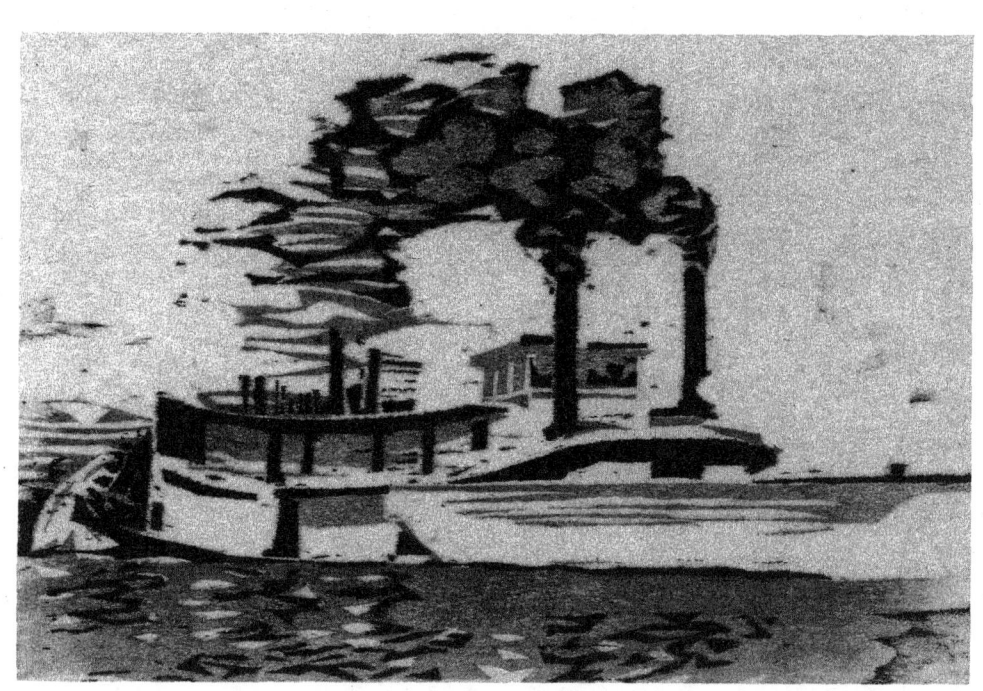

67 Shantyboats at Brent, Kentucky

Christmas card, 1965. Hand signed in ink.

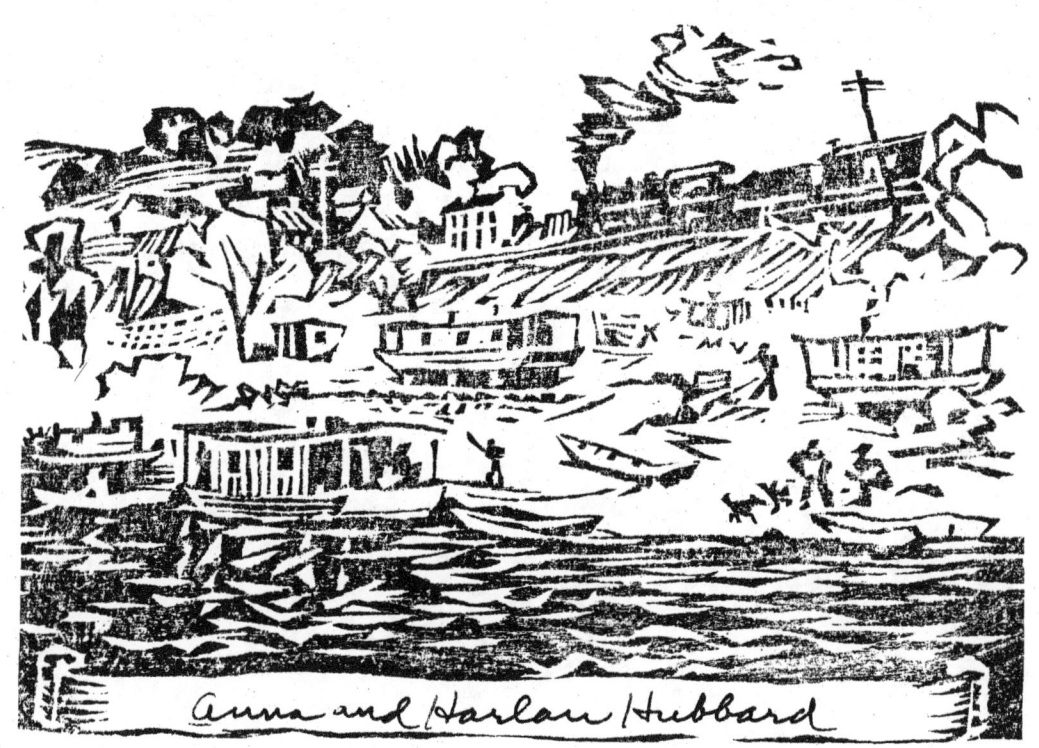

Anna and Harlan Hubbard

68   River with trees
I see before me the river slowly flowing past, quiet,
almost unnoticed, but I feel its power. What can stop it?

August 14, 1935

Journals, 1929-1944, page 116

On HH list. Printed in black and gray.

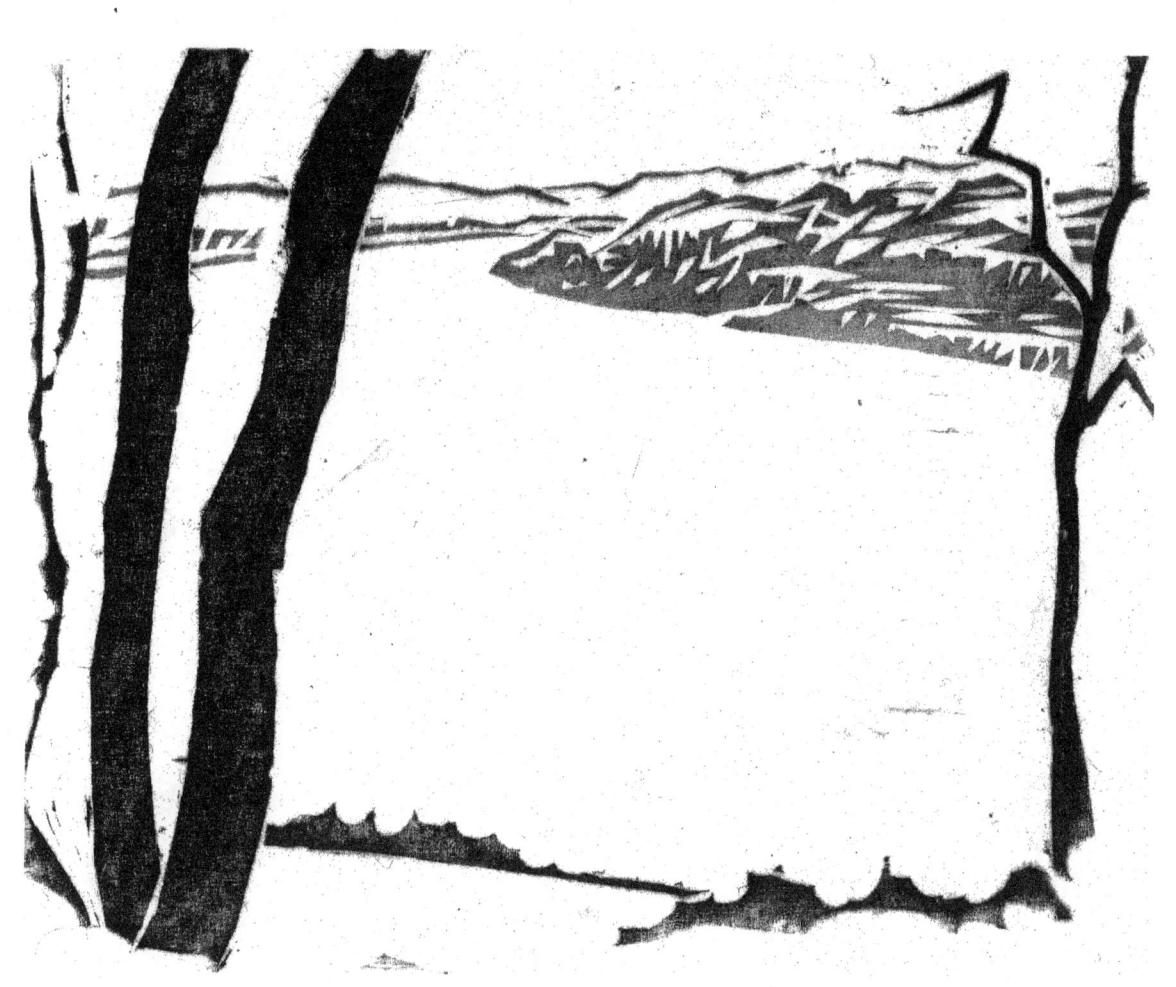

69 Old ferry *Trimble*, Milton, Kentucky, to Madison, Indiana

Christmas card, 1966. One star on HH list. Writing (in ink) not on block.

Old ferry TRIMBLE Milton - Madison

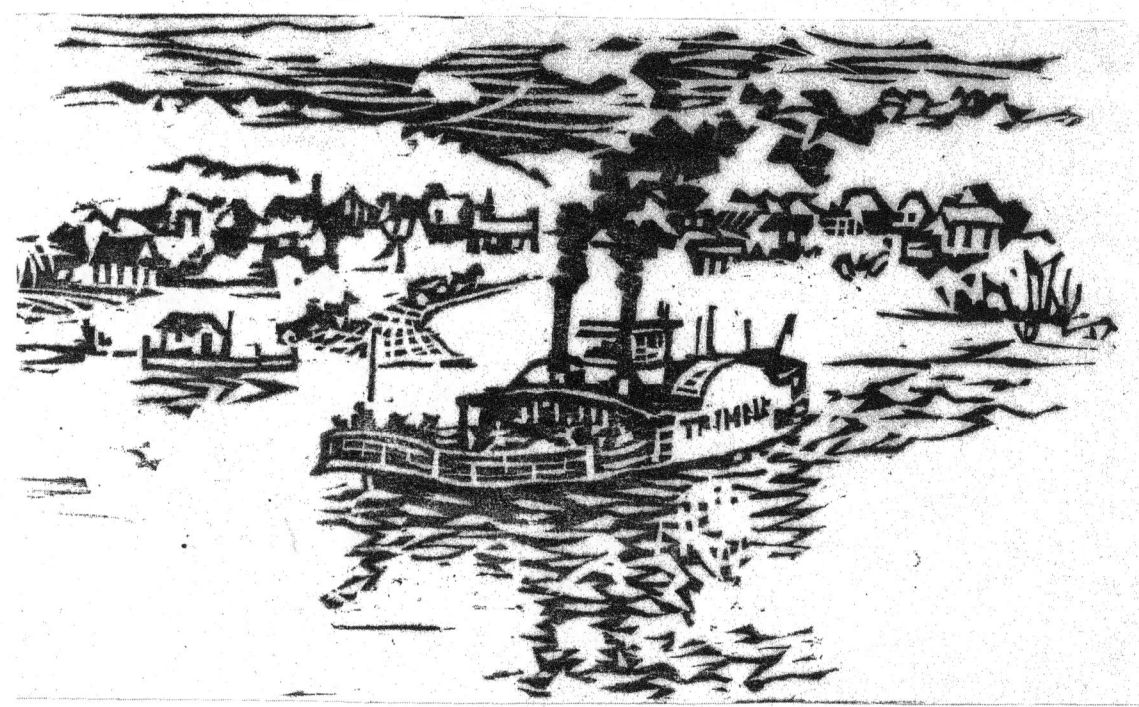

Anna and Harlan Hubbard 1966

70 Barn

This earth is a fit setting for a noble life, for one of peace and joy.

Journal, December 12, 1963

Christmas card, 1967

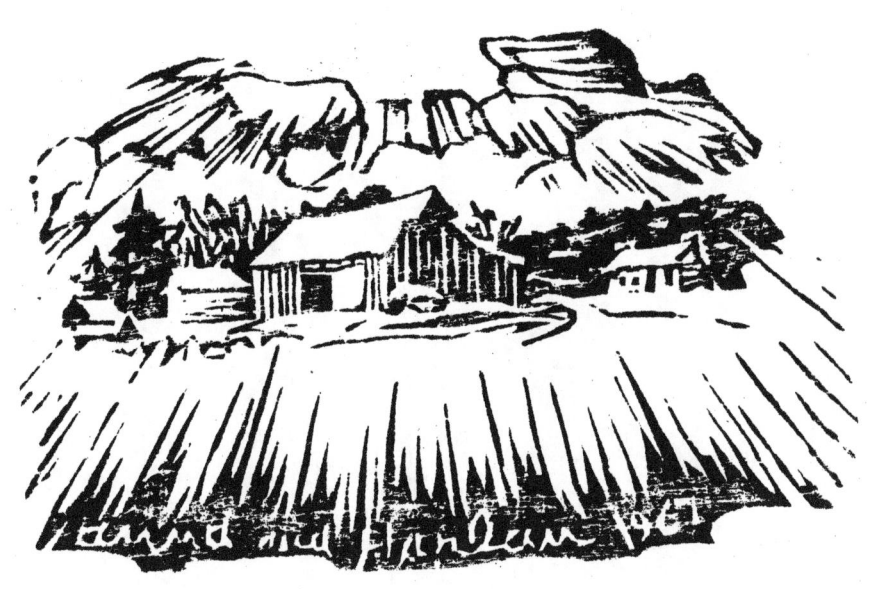

71   River scene with steamboat

Christmas card, 1970.   Hand signed and dated in ink.

Anna and Harlan Hubbard 1970

72 Trees with snow

Christmas card, 1959.   Printed in white ink on dark blue paper.

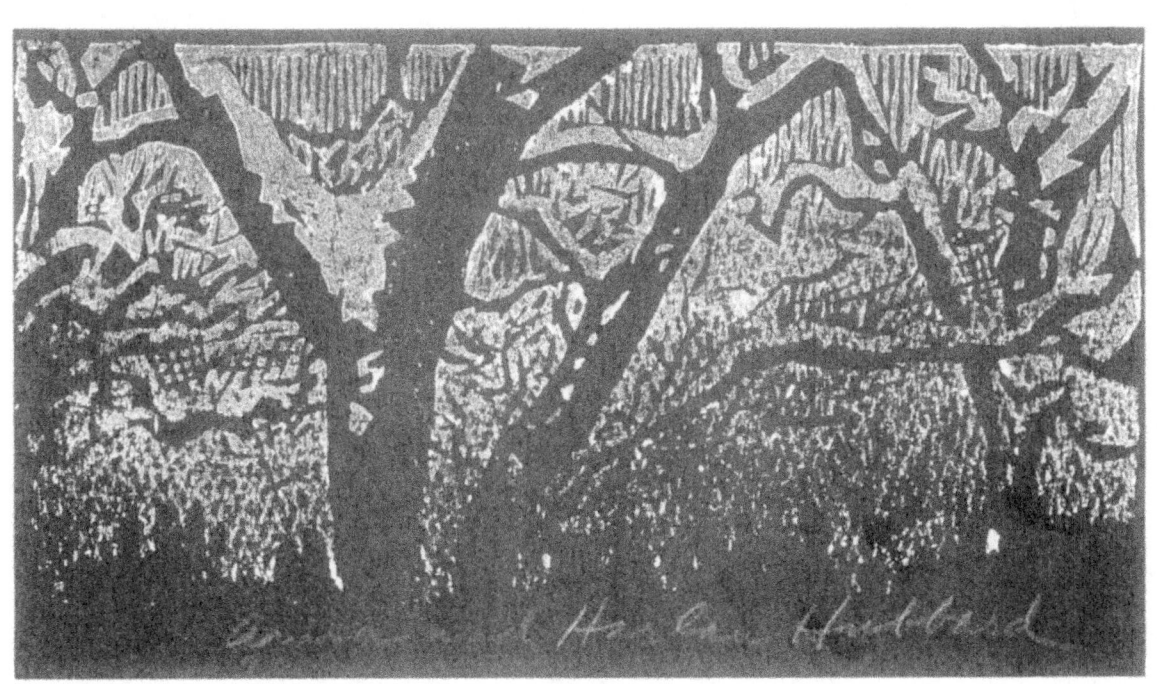

73 Nannygoat and kids

This PM I headed off the goats, or part of them way up the hollow and followed them back to the gate. I like to watch them—who could enjoy the woods more. I wish I could get my living so directly and simply as they do. Theirs is an unhurried peaceful existence, they are cared for, and no effort or concern is required of them.

Journal, October 23, 1961

Christmas card, 1961. Two stars on HH list. Printed in white ink on dark gray paper. Hubbard considered this one of his three best prints, the others being 50 and 51.

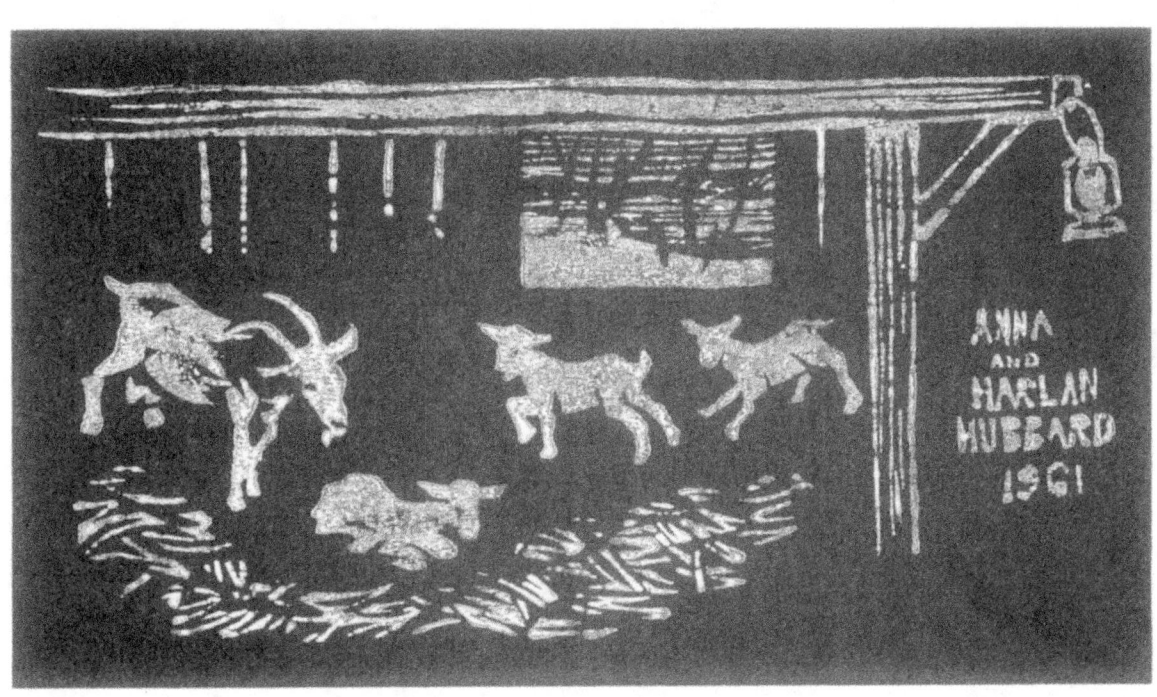

74   Footbridge in Payne Hollow

The other evening, when I stopped on the footbridge and looked down the stony creek bed, between the lines of trees, some tall pale sycamores, toward the river, with a glimpse of the blue hills beyond; I suddenly felt a great love for this place. It has become part of me.

Journal, December 14, 1965

Christmas card, 1982. Hand signed in ink.

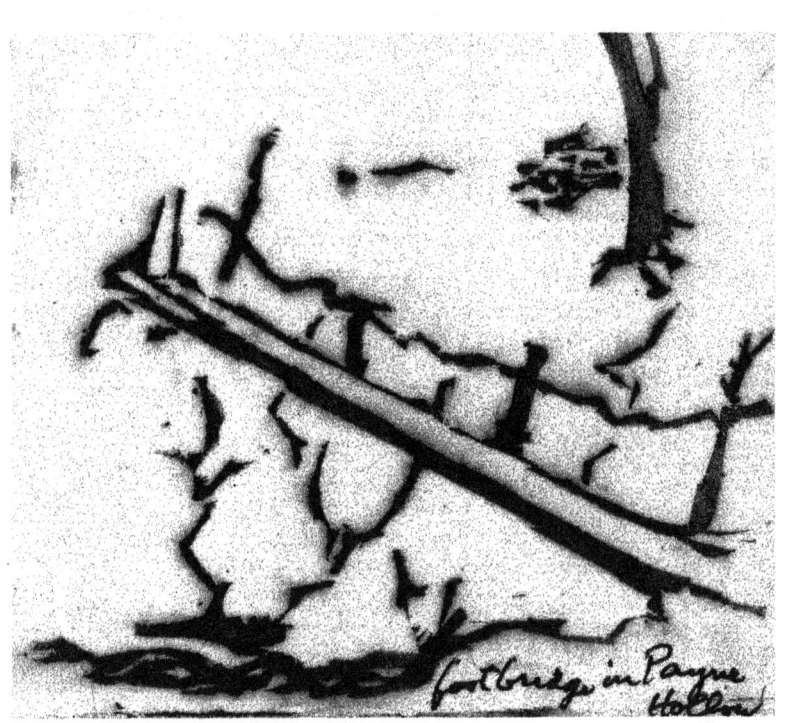

footbridge in Prague
Holland

75   The house at Payne Hollow

To arise in the frosty morning at the point of daybreak, climb the
hill and cut wood, while the sky lightens above the soaring trees;
to eat this wholesome, sweet food, to use my body, hands and
mind at the endless work I have to do; to read by the firelight,
to sleep warm and snug; all this shared and enjoyed by my
loving partner—what manner of a man originated this
idea of a happier life beyond death?

Journal, December 12, 1955

Christmas card, date unknown.

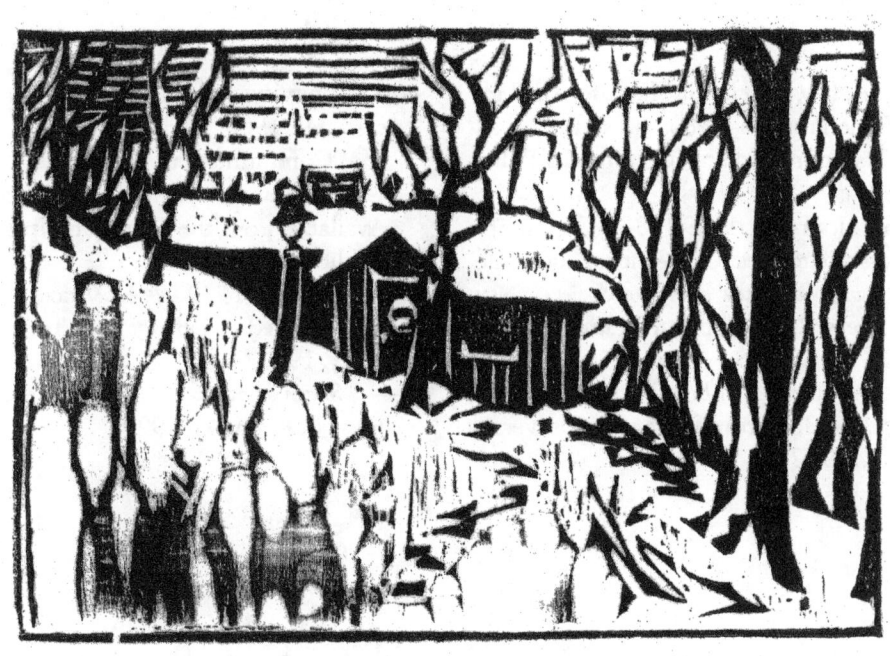

Sources of the Quotations

Burdine, Florence A. Fowler. *Harlan Hubbard: The Man and His Art.* Slide Program, 1980. 80 slides. Available from the Frankfort (Indiana) Community Public Library.

Hubbard, Harlan. Journals, 1929-1987. Typescript. Copy in University Archives, University of Louisville.

——. *Payne Hollow: Life on the Fringe of Society.* New York: Eakins Press, 1974; reprint, Frankfort, Kentucky: Gnomon Press, 1985.

——. *Shantyboat: A River Way of Life.* New York: Dodd, Mead, and Co., 1953; reprint, Lexington: University Press of Kentucky, 1977.

——. Interview with Florence Fowler Burdine. Audiocassette. 1980. Available from the Frankfort (Indiana) Community Public Library.

——. Interview with John Morgan. Audiocassette. 1981. Available from the Frankfort (Indiana) Community Public Library.

——. *Journals, 1929-1944.* Vincent Kohler and David F. Ward, eds. Lexington: University Press of Kentucky, 1987.

——. *Shantyboat on the Bayous.* Lexington: University Press of Kentucky, 1990.

Contributors

Wendell Berry, poet, novelist, and essayist, is well known for his writings on environmental issues. He is author of *Harlan Hubbard: Life and Work*

Florence Fowler Burdine is a painter and potter. She has catalogued the paintings of Harlan Hubbard and produced an accompanying slide program.

Bill Caddell is director of the Frankfort (Indiana) Community Public Library and artistic executor of the Harlan Hubbard estate.

Robert Browning Reed is Professor Emeritus of Art (printmaking) at Purdue University.